HERBERT SCHMIDT

SWORD FIGHTING

AN INTRODUCTION TO HANDLING A LONG SWORD

Schiffer Publishing Ltd

4880 Lower Valley Road • Atglen, PA 19310

Other Schiffer Books on Related Subjects:

Antique Swords & Daggers
Mircea Veleanu
978-0-7643-2506-9. $79.95

Imperial German Edged Weaponry: Volume One: Army and Cavalry
Thomas Johnson with Victor Diehl and Thomas Wittmann
978-0-7643-2934-0. $79.95

Originally published in German by Wieland Verlag GmbH, under the title *Schwertkampf: Der Kampf mit dem langen Schwert nach der Deutschen Schule*

English translation by David Johnston: Photography by Stefan Grdic

Library of Congress Control Number: 2014947890

Type set in ITC Garamond Std/Minion Pro

ISBN: 978-0-7643-4792-4
Printed in China

Published by Schiffer Publishing, Ltd.
4880 Lower Valley Road
Atglen, PA 19310
Phone: (610) 593-1777; Fax: (610) 593-2002
E-mail: Info@schifferbooks.com

For our complete selection of fine books on this and related subjects,
please visit our website at www.schifferbooks.com. You may also write for a free catalog.

This book may be purchased from the publisher. Please try your bookstore first.

We are always looking for people to write books on new and related subjects.
If you have an idea for a book, please contact us at proposals@schifferbooks.com.

Schiffer Publishing's titles are available at special discounts for bulk purchases for sales promotions or premiums. Special editions, including personalized covers, corporate imprints, and excerpts can be created in large quantities for special needs. For more information, contact the publisher.

Contents

CONTENTS

Foreword:
About this Book

After many centuries, the Medieval sword still has the power to fascinate. It is much more than a weapon. It also embodies a time, the Middle Ages, and an idea, knighthood. The ideals of knighthood—honor, justice, fidelity, truthfulness, and defending the weak against the strong—are also closely linked with the sword. The hero can use many weapons, but he certainly carries a sword. We know this from books, movies and, more recently, computer games.

Handling a sword enables us to live out and experience all of these ideas, ideals, and fantasies. That was probably what spurred most of us to become involved with swordfighting in the beginning. But the more deeply and seriously we grapple with the subject of swordfighting, the more we realize that our ideas and ideals are wrong. These fantasies sink more and more into the grave, and in the end almost nothing is left of our original ideas. Instead we gain something else, something more valuable: knowledge.

For each of our naïve ideals we recognize as false, we gain in knowledge. We learn to recognize the real contexts, and at the end of this journey we stand, so to speak, at the other end of the spectrum. Few of our youthful fantasies remain, but they have been replaced by knowledge, understanding, and insight—and with respect to swordfighting, by proficiency and experience. This path from fantasy to reality is absolutely necessary, if you wish to tackle the subject seriously.

The serious seeker wants knowledge, insight and especially proficiency. And so he slaves away in regular training, accepts defeats and plows through medieval manuscripts. He studies illustrations in books, frescoes and paintings. He can be found in museums, castles and libraries. He begins to take an interest in metallurgy and the arts of forging, medicine and architecture. His thirst for knowledge leads him to delve into clothing, tanning, shoemaking, and many other aspects of life in the Middle Ages. He accepts the wounds suffered in free fights with a smile and afterward still reaches for the long knife, the dagger, the pollaxe, and the buckler. He knows that there is much more to swordfighting than working with the blade.

This book is meant to be an introduction to handling the long sword. To be able to compile a book about so complex a subject as swordfighting, it is first necessary to define the area and set clear boundaries. This book therefore deals solely with handling the long sword, in keeping with the German School in the tradition of Johannes Liechtenauer. Its focus is the interpretation of earlier sources. At the same time, I have attempted to orientate myself toward the acceptable modern forms with respect to nomenclature and techniques. I have intentionally avoided delving into details in this book. I am fully aware that the guards, cuts and techniques have undergone development. I am also aware that very many differences are to be found in the sources. The purpose of this book, therefore, is to enable those with an interest to get started in swordfighting with the long sword and convey the basic techniques.

The old masters were wont to divide up their combat manuals in sometimes incomprehensible ways. I have intentionally broken with this. I think that the form I have selected is easier to understand. The techniques illustrated here have been taken from various combat manuals—purists may forgive me if I do not offer the source with every technique. In the text I have completely dispensed with naming sources. If anyone is interested in these sources—most are now available on the internet—he can find them in the bibliography in the appendix. Any questions will surely be answered competently by any serious club. A list of such clubs can also be found at the end of the book.

The techniques explained herein should be viewed as tools. Each technique learned is one more tool in your toolbox. In combat we face each other in certain situations and then choose the tool that seems best suited to decide this situation, this combat, in our favor. Some tools are very specialized, others are very versatile. The more techniques you master, the more possibilities are open to you. For this reason, I have avoided linking techniques in certain fixed sequences. The combination of individual techniques makes up a large part of each fighter's style and is an expression of his personality.

It is impossible to explain all the subtleties and additional steps to the techniques in a book. That is one of the reasons why no book can replace an instructor. Training with another person is absolutely necessary in swordfighting, which is a confrontation with another. But with this book, those without a club in their vicinity can make a beginning themselves and, with others, delve deeper into the fascinating world of swordfighting.

I have tried to make the text as understandable as possible. Nevertheless, while reading, should you stumble across an expression you do not understand, you can turn to the glossary at the end of the book.

A book like this is always a joint effort. Even if there is just one author behind it, that author has practiced, fought, discussed and learned with many others. So many opinions and views flow into it. That is even more so of me, as I actively sought the opinions of others. I did this, not just to avoid mistakes, but also to grasp the current state of the Central-European swordfighting scene. Dozens of combats, seminars, and weekends have left their marks on me, and today I am still grateful to everyone who showed me my limits and errors with so many blue marks. In this respect, this book is a child of many parents; however, I can only write through the filter of my own opinion and understanding. I am therefore solely responsible for any errors in this book.

The reconstruction of historical swordfighting is in a state of constant development—and that is a good thing. There are surely those whose opinions differ from some of the statements made in this book. Another fighter would undoubtedly have explained this or that technique differently. Another would have distributed the emphasis differently. I may, however, assume that the fundamentals presented here are sound. Even if there are differences in the interpretation of techniques, the book as a whole is certainly suitable for learning swordfighting on a sound basis. I also hope that this book generates discussions of all kinds and in this way enlivens and perhaps even furthers historical swordfighting.

There are some people without whom I would never have been in a position to write such a book. First I would like to tank all the members of Ars Gladii, who gave me the opportunity to learn so much. Many people within—but also outside—the historical swordfighting scene helped me along. I would especially like to thank Dieter Bachmann, Jörg Bellinghausen, Matt Easton, Martin Enzi, Peter Johnsson, Thomas Laible, Rachel Miller, Bernhard Müller, Wolfgang Ritter, Chris Stride, Oliver Walter, Roland Warzecha, Phillipe Willaume and Christian Wolf.

Unfortunately, I cannot name everyone to whom I am grateful for assistance by dueling with me, discussing or sharing their opinions. I will therefore thank the clubs of which they are members: Boars Tooth, De Taille et d'Estoc, Dreynschlag, Freywild, Hammaborg, Klingenspiel, Ochs, Rittersporn, Schola Gladiatoria, School of Medieval Fencing, Zornhau.

I would also like to offer special thanks to the photographer, Stefan Grdic, along with photo models Gabi Ammann, Claudia Gmeiner, Berko Husejnovic and Bernhard Müller (all four of Ars Gladii) for their patience in front of and behind the camera.

Last but not least, many thanks to Harald Winter for his valuable encouragement and patience. Without him this book would contain many more errors. Special thanks also to Caroline Wydeau for her layout, her help, and especially her humor. Finally, many thanks to Hans Joachim Wieland for unhesitatingly diving into this venture.

I hope that you enjoy reading this book and as well, of course, training.

The author may be reached by way of the Ars Gladii Swordfighting Club website (www.arsgladii.at) and by email at info@arsgladii.at.

Introduction:
Definitions

Historical European sword combat—what, in fact, is that? If we examine the definition more closely, then it becomes more clear to us which requirements apply.

Historical: The word indicates that we are dealing with verifiable technologies and materials. It is necessary, therefore, for followers to adhere as closely as possible to the verifiable techniques and materials and, to the extent possible, also attempt to tailor their fighting style to the historical facts and customs. Techniques are judged with respect to old conditions and clothing, and not as to whether they would be effective in the modern environment. The primary sources are combat manuals, and all sources must be verifiable.

European: This term is self-explanatory. In some cases the borders are fluid, as they apply to the difference between Eastern and Western Europe.

Sword Combat: This term is also self-explanatory, but it is deserving of clarification. It concerns the handling of a sword as part of a fighting system. In principle, all kinds of swords are included—daggers, rapiers, long swords, single-handed swords. Viewed historically, sword combat is a part of the general martial arts. In addition to sword combat, wrestling was practiced as well as combat with a multitude of other weapons (pike weapons, dusacks, long knives, daggers and others).

To summarize: Historical European sword combat is combat with the European sword utilizing the researchable fighting systems of bygone eras.

In this book I will further limit the field, restricting the weapon to the long sword, the time period to the 15th and 16th centuries, and the geographical area to German-speaking Central Europe. Strictly speaking, the book, therefore, deals with the historical combat using the long sword following the German school, in the tradition of Liechtenauer.

It is important to note here that the above-named premises should always be kept in the back of the mind—especially the requirement for verifiable techniques. Of course, gaps always arise in reconstruction. I have attempted to close these while staying as close to the existing system as possible.

There is a marked difference between historical sword combat and the stage or show battles that we often see at medieval fairs, on stage, and, not least, in motion pictures. These show combats usually have nothing in common with true sword combat. The phenomenon of the show combat is not new, for we have proof of such show fighters from the 14th century, whose acts were designed to appeal to the public. Then as now, serious fighters did not have a great deal of sympathy for these show fighters, especially when these prided themselves as good fighters or tried to make the audiences believe that they were masters of special techniques.

In Cod. HS 3227a of 1389 (see more on sources in Chapter 3) we find the following passage: *But I would like to see one who devises and executes a technique or stroke that does not come from Liechtenauer's artistry.*

Fencing masters of the day thus state quite explicitly (especially the author of HS 3227a) that the fighting artistry of Johannes Liechtenauer contains everything, or at least that everything could be derived from it. When one considers that many fencing masters, including career fighters, based their techniques on the teachings of Liechtenauer, then one recognizes that these teachings represent a comprehensive and above all practical system.

This also outlines the biggest difference between historical sword combat and show fighting: amusing the public is not important. It is also not about looking good. It is all about winning a sword combat as efficiently and quickly as possible. To achieve this, we follow the masters from the time when such combats were a matter of life and death. Historical fighting is not appealing to the public, as it if often over too quickly. The spectator understands little of what is happening. Instead, the techniques are designed to overcome the opponent with as few movements as possible and the least possible expenditure of energy.

Weaponry:
A Specialized Device

The history of the European sword is long and varied. Its origins are lost in the darkness of prehistory, and even today more is being added. What interests us in this book is the history of the long sword. This long sword has many names, but the term "long sword" has become customary in professional circles.

The long sword appeared in the first half of the 14th century and remained into the 17th century, and in isolated cases the 19th century. Its heyday was the 15th and 16th centuries. The long sword developed from the single-handed sword, wielded in one hand. The grip became longer and enabled the weapon to be wielded in two hands. Along with the grip, the guard also became larger. Sometimes the old blade was simply remounted, resulting in a long sword with the blade of a single-handed sword. In most cases, however, a new weapon was made.

We are all familiar with the general appearance of a typical long sword from the early 15th century: straight guard, a disc or bulb pommel, long grip and a very massive blade. The weapon became more and more refined, however, and finally achieved what

was probably its optimal form at the end of the 15th century. The blade became more pointed and tapered. The result was a sword that was not only very fast and maneuverable, but which also had outstanding blade tip control. Nevertheless, the cut was very good, and the weapon was obviously designed for an expert. Those familiar with the Oakeshott typology will recognize these sword forms in the Types XVa, XVIa, XVII and XVIIIa and b.

The very pointed blade shape also makes the sword suitable for use against an armored opponent. Striking plate armor with a sword at best results in dents in the armor. One must instead try to stab at the unprotected areas. Such targets include the inner sides of elbows and knees, armpits, crotch, visor, and palms of the hands. In doing so, chain mail often has to be pierced. Using half-sword techniques (in which one hand grips and guides the blade, see Page 32) the long sword is converted into a kind of lance for attacking these unprotected areas. The pommel and guard were also used against an armored opponent. The long sword as it appeared in the late 15th century was thus a multifunctional weapon, for use against both armored and unarmored opponents.

SWORD NOMENCLATURE

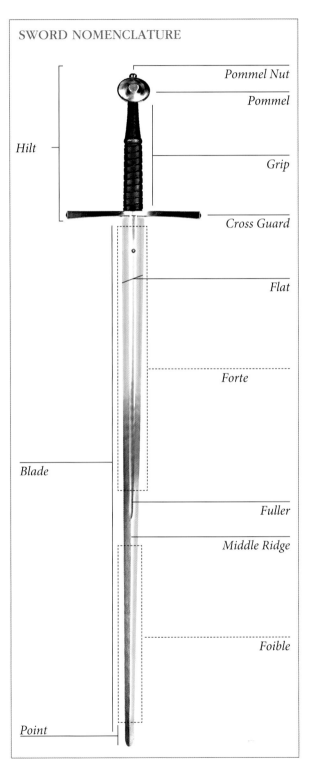

Hilt

Pommel Nut

Pommel

Grip

Cross Guard

Flat

Forte

Blade

Fuller

Middle Ridge

Foible

Point

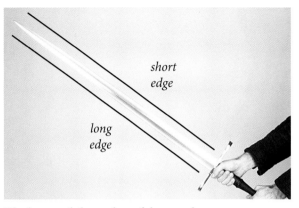

short edge

long edge

The long and short edges of the sword.

NODAL POINTS

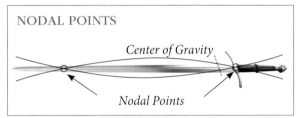

Center of Gravity

Nodal Points

Holy Catherine by Lucas Cranach, ca. 1516.

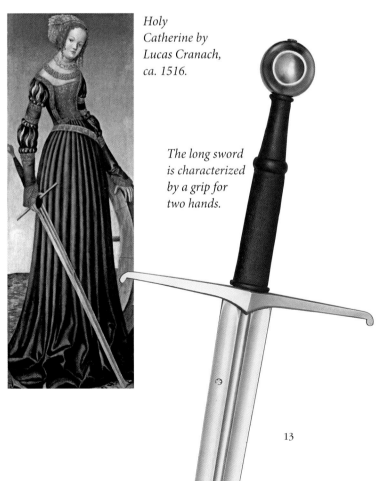

The long sword is characterized by a grip for two hands.

13

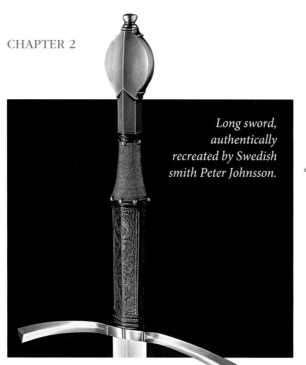

Long sword, authentically recreated by Swedish smith Peter Johnsson.

Modern interpretation of a long sword by Herbert Schmidt.

Another long sword by Peter Johnsson.

Combat with the long sword is a duel between two opponents. In the broader sense it also includes combat against several opponents, as for example might happen in the event of an ambush on a country road. Quite clearly not included, however, is combat on the battlefield. This book will deal only with combat between fighters without armor—so-called "*Bloßfechten*" (fighting without armor). As this involves two fighters who join combat at a specified time and place, much more skill can flow into the battle. That, in turn, encourages the use of specialized weapons which are designed to support skilled combat.

Contrary to popular opinion, the sword was not manufactured by one person alone. Specialization and division of work were employed even in the Middle Ages. The blade was made by a smith. Then the blade went to a *Schwertfeger* (Medieval term for a weapons smith), who polished and sharpened it. Most completed blades were sold to dealers, who put them in their stores. They were then selected by a customer and a suitable mounting ordered. These mountings were also made by special smiths, before everything was assembled.

Of course, it also happened that a customer specified a particular smith when ordering a certain blade or sword. In general, the customer bought his sword from a dealer and not from a smith. Blades were traded and often covered great distances. For example, German blades found their way to Scotland, where they were mounted in keeping with local practices.

The sword was and is a special weapon for a special purpose. Of course, a well-made sword will hold up to some use, but it is basically a delicate device. The edges are very sharp and correspondingly fragile. If a blow from another sword is parried with the blade at a static 90° angle, then the opponent's sword digs into the blade and leaves behind a hateful and dangerous nick. This is dangerous, because such a nick represents a predetermined breaking point subjected to significantly greater stress. A sword is not intended for chopping wood, digging in the earth, breaking stones, or being driven through planks. The purpose of a sword is to cut and to stab the enemy. The functions of the sword also include parrying, redirecting, and otherwise manipulating the opponent's sword, but never in such a way that the edge takes the entire force. Use of the sword naturally results in nicks, dulling and other kinds of damage. This is shown to us by many preserved swords in museums and collections that have nicks or that have had such nicks ground out.

Another important aspect is the length of use of a sword. A normal sword combat, as occurred in a trial by combat, was of very brief duration. Even if the sword was used for self-defense, as on a trip, then the fight was not long. One can thus assume that, during a sword's entire period of use, it was employed for perhaps several minutes, and in the worst case hours. A modern training sword as used by clubs these days is subjected to much more use. Often the user trains twice a week. Then there are weekend seminars and special exhibitions. One can thus safely assume that a modern training sword is subject to many times the stress of a sword in the Middle Ages, even if we include use of the sword in war.

When purchasing a sword, be sure that it really is intended for training. Cheap and unsuitable swords are not only too heavy and often unbalanced, they are also prone to breaking and are thus dangerous. Clean technique is almost impossible with such a sword, as the poor balance and weight are hindrances.

Therefore, stay clear of a sword that is made too heavy and massive. It may appear indestructible, but one can not fight with it. Good workmanship, good balance, and an authentic weight are important. More on this in chapter 17.

The Sources:
Testimonials from a Turbulent Time

The heyday of the German School was the 15th century. The most important combat manuals were written at that time, and fighting schools were established. The late Middle Ages were characterized by drastic revolutions in almost every aspect of contemporary life. War was waged somewhere practically all of the time. Despite this, brilliant cultural achievements were also made.

The 15th century witnessed many important events. Johannes Gensfleisch (Gutenberg) was born in 1400. In 1415 the English won the Battle of Agincourt. In July of the same year, Jan Hus (John Huss) was burned at the Council of Constance, even though he had been guaranteed safe conduct. The result was the Hussite Wars, which lasted until 1436. At about the same time, from 1418 to 1436, Filippo Brunelleschi built the dome of the Florentine cathedral, Santa Maria del Fiore. The last crowning of a Holy Roman emperor in Rome took place in 1452, when Frederick III was crowned by Pope Nicholas V. It was the same year that Gutenberg, with a credit of 800 guilders, began printing the Bible, and Leonardo da Vinci was born. One year later the Hundred Years War, which had been going on since 1337, ended, and the Turks conquered Constantinople. Two years later, in 1455, the War of the Roses began for the crown of England. The houses of York and Lancaster waged bitter warfare until 1485. In 1487, Bartolomeu Diaz sailed around the southern tip of Africa for the first time, and the Hexenhammer (*Malleus Maleficarum*, or the hammer of the witches) was written. Granada fell in 1492, marking the end of the *Reconquista*. A new campaign began in the same year with Columbus's discovery of America.

Maximillian I, also known as "the last knight," became regent in 1493. Five years later, in 1498, Vasco de Gama set foot in India. In 1499, the century came to an end with victory by the Swiss in the Swabian wars, in which they secured de facto independence from the Holy Roman Empire.

The most important combat manuals were written against this historical background. As the goal of historical European sword fighting is to reconstruct the martial arts of the Middle Ages, naturally we must adhere to the sources that still survive. The earliest sources from which a fighting system can be derived come from the German language. The oldest surviving combat manual is the I.33. It dates roughly from the year 1300 and describes combat with the single-handed sword and buckler. The next combat manual appeared in 1389 and is known as HS 3227a. It follows the tradition of Johannes Liechtenauer, the father figure of the German school.

Unfortunately, we know very little about Johannes Liechtenauer. He lived in the 14th century and apparently travelled widely in Europe in order to perfect his craft. He left behind his knowledge in so-called "mneumonic verses." These mneumonic verses were intentionally composed cryptically, in order to keep the skills secret and not generally accessible. Liechtenauer's successors later began writing down his mneumonic verses and explaining them. These works form the basis of our reconstruction of how to handle the long sword. The name "Liechtenauer" later became a sort of seal of quality, and many fencing masters embellished their teaching by tracing it back to Liechtenauer.

The most important combat manuals, which were consulted in writing this book, are:

HS 3227a	1389
Sigmund Ringeck	1440
Hans Talhoffer	1443, 1459, 1467
Jud Lew	1450
Peter von Danzig	1452
Paulus Kal	1460
Hans von Speyer	1491
Solothurner Fechtbuch	1500
Codex Wallerstein	1556

There are also many other combat manuals. Most were written in Early New High German. There is thus also a linguistic barrier between us and the learning of swordfighting of the late Middle Ages. The first step in reconstruction therefore consists of transcription. After transcription, we have a readable text, albeit in Early New High German. Here is an excerpt from the combat manual HS 3227a of 1389:

"… wen dir eiyner czu hewt / mit eynen obirhaw / so saltu du keyn im weder hawen den czornhaw also das dir mit dyme ort vaste keyn im schisset / …"

[Roughly: *when someone strikes an upper strike [Oberhaw] / against you, then you shall / strike a rage strike [Czornhaw] at him; that is, thrust your point fast towards him.*]

The same section of text from Sigmund Ringeck's combat manual of 1440, roughly 50 years later:

"Daß vernym also: wann dir ainer von siner rechten sytten oben ein hawet, so haw einen zorn haw mitt der langen schniden och von diner rechten achseln mitt im starck ein. Ist er dann waich am schwert, so schüß jm den ort für sich lang ein zuo dem gesicht. Vnnd träw im zuo stechen."

[Roughly: *When your adversary strikes at you from his right side with a strike from above (Oberhau), then hit with a strike of wrath from your right shoulder against it. Strike with your true edge strongly. When he is weak at the sword then, thrust into his face along his blade. Threaten him with a thrust.*]

Foreword to the interpretation by fencing master Sigmund Ringeck of Liechtenauer's mneumonic verses.

A page from the I.33 manual ca. 1300.

These combat manuals are read, the individual techniques summarized, and then the actual interpretation begins. With the combat manual and one or more training partners, the individual sections of text are then translated into techniques. In doing so, one repeatedly checks to see if one is adhering precisely to the text. If one is of the opinion that he has found the correct interpretation, then this technique is put to the test in a free fight. Only if a technique follows the text of the combat manual, works, and is proven in a free fight, is it demonstrated to other fighters at international meets. If, after thorough testing, it is found to be sound, it can be regarded as accepted. The techniques of the German School were also worked out this way in the last decades. They are, for the most part, considered confirmed.

Of course, not every technique is examined in this way; instead, parts of the system are worked out and repeatedly gone through with various fighters, and compared and adjusted a little here and there, until an optimal result is achieved. Of course, constant criticism is received from all sides during the process. This also helps to confirm the high standard that historical combat has achieved in Europe today.

The techniques illustrated in this book all come from combat manuals and are verifiable; but in some cases the fundamentals are an exception, as the sword fighting masters transmitted the fundamentals directly to their students and did not include them in their written records. The techniques reveal themselves implicitly through the depictions and also through the interjected remarks of some of the masters. The techniques are congruent with the system of the masters of the German School.

The majority of the conveyed techniques have their origins in the 15th century. They have a long tradition and in some cases can be traced far back. From the context, it is obvious that there was already a highly-developed culture of sword fighting in Central Europe long before its heyday in the 15th century.

Unfortunately for us, no earlier combat manuals have survived, but there are more than enough clues in Medieval literature, in which heroes who knew how to fight skillfully are praised. Individual "*Schirmschläge*" (defensive blows) are also mentioned. The word "*schirmen*" originally meant "to defend," but eventually it also came to be used as a general term meaning "to engage in swordplay" or "to engage in combat."

The following appears in the Gudrunlied (roughly 1230-1240):

*Des küneges ingesinde ze hove schilde truoc
kiule und buckelaere, geschirmet wart dâ gnuoc,
gevohten mit den swerten, mit gabilôte geschozzen
vil ûf guote schilde, die jungen helde wâren unverdrozzen
(Kudrun 356, 1-4)*

Wate stuont in huote, / same r ein kemphe wære' …
(360, 3-4)

…die mînen slege viere', … (362, 3)

Or else in the Edelstein of 1349:

*… ez dröut mit worten manig man
der doch Wenig schirmen kann. (Der Edelstein – Ulrich Boner) …*

And even in Tristan (1210) by Gottfried von Straßburg we find:

*… wol schirmen, starke ringen,
wol loufen, sere springen,
dar zuo schiezen den schaft (Tristan 2113-15)*

It is not difficult to find clues in the literature of the Middle Ages that combat was very skillful and had very little to do with crude, aimless violence. The combat manuals and the martial arts handed down by them are the legacy of this long tradition. The roots of these books thus reach far back into the past.

A page from a combat manual by Albrecht Dürer from about 1520.

A table from a combat manual by Hans Talhoffer, circa 1467.

A page from the combat manual by Joachim Meyer, circa 1600.

The Foundation:
Fundamentals of Fighting Technique

4.1 Holding the Weapon

The long sword is gripped with the right hand (by a right-hander) directly below the guard. This allows the thumb to lie on, over or under the guard. Many fighters prefer a grip with some distance between the guard and the index finger. In certain techniques this reduces the danger of the index finger being cut. The left hand grips the sword below the right. Here there are several possibilities: the left hand can be positioned directly against the right, or it can lie directly under the pommel or partly on the pommel. One can also completely enclose the pommel. All of these grip styles are correct and historically verified. Here it is personal preference that decides. Basically one can react more quickly if one grips the pommel with the left hand. On the other hand, if the hands are closer together the blow is more powerful. I personally advise gripping the pommel, so as to gain the maximum possible leverage.

Depending on movement and technique, the thumb is placed on the blade surface. I characterize this as "thumb grip" or "thumb on the flat." In certain postures the thumb grip offers more power and better control of the blade, and some techniques are only possible if it is used.

One can also place the index finger over the guard. This "fingering" should only be used, however, if the weapon has a hilt (with parrying rings) that protects this finger. Otherwise it can very quickly result in serious injury to, or, in the worst case, loss of the finger.

The sword should be held loosely but controlled. In many techniques the hands move on and around the grip. The sword is often turned in the left or right hand. When swinging or thrusting, not until just before the strike is the grip tightened, thus fixing the sword and arm. Of course the sword should not be held so loosely that one loses it or it can be knocked out of one's hand.

4.2 Footwork

Very little is said about footwork in the combat manuals, but what is mentioned is of great importance. There are a number of steps that result from the techniques and the directions of motion. No consensus has yet formed as to the names of these steps, but the terms used here have in some cases become common usage.

In the basic posture one stands with feet about shoulder width apart, the left leg forward, the right back. The right leg is angled slightly outwards, the left positioned so that the toes face the opponent. Weight is equally distributed on both legs, one stands with the knees slightly bent. The center of gravity is kept rather low and central over the legs. In this position (scales) one's stance is stable and yet one can move fluidly in any direction. From this stance the Guards are taken.

HALF STEP (*Halbschritt*):
The half step involves talking one step forward with the front leg. The back leg remains where it is. In a half step to the rear, the front leg remains stationary, and the back leg steps back.

The wide grip: the left hand covers the pommel. Because of this, the great leverage makes it possible to react very quickly.

The closer grip: the left hand is just below the right. This automatically makes the blows more powerful.

Hand position in the left Plow (more on the Guards beginning on Page 34): the thumb is on the flat, and the sword is turned in the right hand. The right wrist is straight and not bent.

Hand position in the Ox, with the thumb on the flat: here the thumb supports the blade and provides greater stability. Here, too, the wrist should be kept as straight as possible.

BASIC POSITION OF THE FEET WITH CENTER OF GRAVITY

Front leg points in the direction of the opponent

Center of gravity

The basic posture, also called the Scales by some fencing masters. The knees are slightly bent and are not in line.

ADJUSTMENT STEP

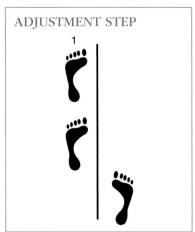

ADJUSTMENT STEP

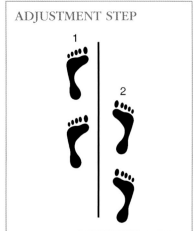

CHANGE STEP

FULL STEP

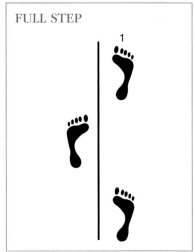

ADJUSTMENT STEP (*Nachstellschritt*):
In the adjustment step, a step if first taken with the front leg, followed by the back leg. The same basic stance is taken at the end of the movement. If the adjustment step is carried out to the rear, then the back leg moves back first, followed by the front leg.

CHANGE STEP (*Wechselschritt*):
In the change step, the legs change their position. The front leg moves back, the back leg forwards. The body keeps its position during the movement.

FULL STEP (CHANGE OF STANCE)
(*Ganzer Schritt OR Auslagenwechsel*):
A normal step, as in walking. If the left was in front, after the step the right leg is in front.

CROSS STEP (*Kreuzschritt*):
In the cross step, one steps out of line. The back leg crosses over the front leg to the side. The direction of movement is to the side of the front leg. The (formerly) front leg is then moved back, as can be seen in the illustration. At the end, one is standing at an angle to the opponent with the other leg forward. If one begins with the right leg forward, one ends with the left leg in front.

DOUBLE STEP (*Doppelter Schritt*):
The double step takes place in the same manner as the cross step. The back leg steps to the side and becomes the front leg. Here, however, the direction of movement is to the side of the back leg.

TRANSLATION STEP (*Übersetzschritt*):
In the Translation Step, one takes a full step, immediately followed by another. At the end, one is in the same basic stance, but two steps closer to the opponent.

All of these steps naturally work both forwards and backwards and should be practiced in both directions. Always try to maintain as upright and centered a posture as possible. This will enable you to react better, have better power delivery and better balance.

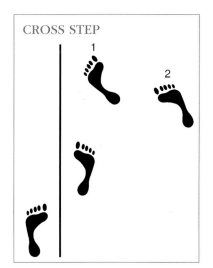

CROSS STEP

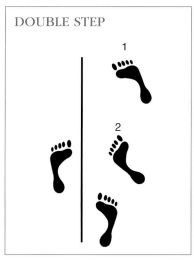

DOUBLE STEP

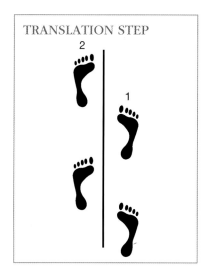

TRANSLATION STEP

4.3 Correct Striking

One can do three things with the sword blade: strike, thrust, cut. These three basic functions were at one time called the "three wonders." All well and good, but how does one do them correctly?

THE STRIKE/BLOW:
A properly executed strike not only hits, it also cuts. In this way one achieves a significantly higher degree of effectiveness. The simplest variant looks like this: we place ourselves in the basic stance, left leg forward, the sword held to the right of the head (Roof Guard, see Chapter 5). Then the right hand with the sword moves forward powerfully in a quadrant towards the target. The left hand uses the grip as a lever and swings the blade forward.

Meanwhile we take a step forward. At the moment the blade strikes, we rotate the hips, and with the body movement we direct the sword downwards and left. We thus achieve a quick and powerful blow, which is drawn on impact. This causes the blade to cut deeper into the target. When striking the blow, one should always be sure to strike through the target and not on the target. Even if the target is standing somewhat farther away and we stretch out our arms to increase range, at the end the sword should again be returned to one of the hanging positions.

The following basically applies to every strike: if striking from the right, then we take a step forward with the right leg or a step back with the left leg. The strikes should be delivered forcefully. We receive the necessary force when we use the grip as a lever and bring the body motion and rotation into the strike. One should never draw back, for by doing so one prematurely reveals one's intentions to the opponent. The force of the blow thus results from a combination of arm and body movement and using the grip as a lever.

THE CUT:
We can cut whenever our blade strikes the opponent. The blade is simply pushed forward (pushed cut) or pulled back (pulled cut).

THE THRUST:
The thrust is simply a linear forward movement of the blade. It is always important to thrust through the target. This point often receives less than adequate consideration because of safety concerns during training. A thrust does not end at the target, rather behind the target. Likewise, if possible the thrust should not be executed with the arms only, but with the entire body. In this way one lends more mass and force to the thrust.

One can thrust from any position. Basically, however, one differentiates between a thrust from below and a thrust from above. In the thrust from below, one stabs upwards from below, for example from the Plow Guard. In the thrust from above, one stabs from above, for example from the Ox Guard. When making the thrust, it is important to move the arms first and only then follow with the body. As a result, the thrust will both be quicker and more effective.

Correct striking: beginning position.

The grip is used as a lever: this helps generate power for the strike.

Middle of the strike movement: the hand guides the movement, the leg follows.

The two variants of the cut: the pushed and the pulled cut.

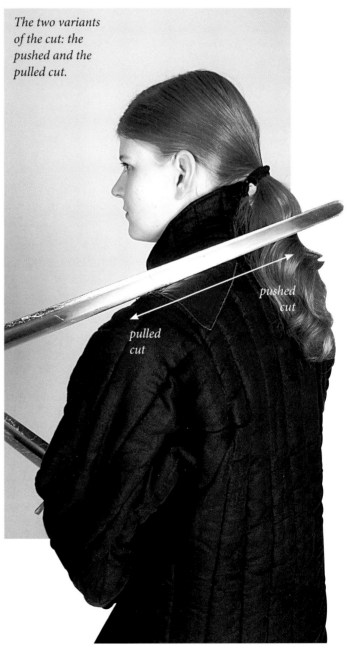

End of the strike movement: on contact the blade is also pulled back and thus cuts.

Correct striking: strike from above without drawing back.

After the strike impacts, the sword is pulled back for additional cutting effect.

The starting position for this under-cut is the Plow.

When thrusting, the arms move first, the body follows.

The thrust from above is mainly executed from the Ox.

Thrust from above from the Ox: in this photo the delivery is too far forward. As a result, balance is affected, which the opponent can exploit to his advantage.

Measure (Mensur): The measure is the distance between two fighters, There are four basic measures:

- *Wide measure: here two steps are required to reach the opponent.*
- *Medium measure: here the opponent can be reached with one step.*
- *Close measure: here no steps are required to reach the opponent. It is not yet possible, however, to reach the opponent with the hand.*
- *Tight measure: here the opponent can be touched with the hands without taking a step. Wrestling takes place in the tight range.*

In the Bind: If the blades touch, then one is a bind or binding position. Usually the Bind is held for short periods. Various techniques are executed from the Bind. The Bind is also the moment of feeling. Many fencing masters viewed the techniques executed in a Bind as the core of the fighting art and described the combat that took place In the Bind as "noble warfare."

Feeling: In the Bind, a fighter analyses the blade's direction of force, position of the point, positioning of the hands, balance and position of the opponent. Subsequent decisions are based on the information gained. Together with the Before/Meanwhile/After, Feeling forms the theoretical basis of sword fighting. Feeling takes place in the Bind or the Talking Window.

Hanging: In the Hanging position, the sword is held so that the point aims down at the opponent's face (upper hanging) or the pommel hangs towards the ground (lower hanging). In all four Hanging positions it is important that the point is aimed at the opponent's face. There are four different Hanging positions: right and left lower and right and left upper.

CHAPTER 4

Half-Sword (Halbschwert): In the Half-Sword, the blade is held with the left hand, roughly in the middle. This grip gives one better control over the point and enables very powerful leverage and thrusting techniques. The Half-Sword is mainly used against an opponent in armor.

BASIC TECHNICAL TERMS

In sword fighting, it is best if certain technical terms are defined. The fencing masters recognized this in the Middle Ages and used an entire range of technical terms. Others were added and adopted later. The most important are:

Over-Cut (Oberhau): *Every strike that is struck from above. Usually an over-cut also strikes above the belt line, but a strike from above on a leg is also an over-cut.*

Under-Cut (Unterhau): *Every strike that is struck from below. Here it depends exclusively on the strike direction.*
An under-cut is struck from below and can strike the legs, but just as well the armpit or the head.

Middle Cut (Mittelhau): *The middle cut is struck horizontally with the long edge. Usually the strike plane is at belly or chest height.*

Opening: *An opening is a fighter's unprotected spot. Of course a fighter cannot move without revealing one or more openings. Openings can also be used intentionally as an invitation, to tempt the opponent to attack.*

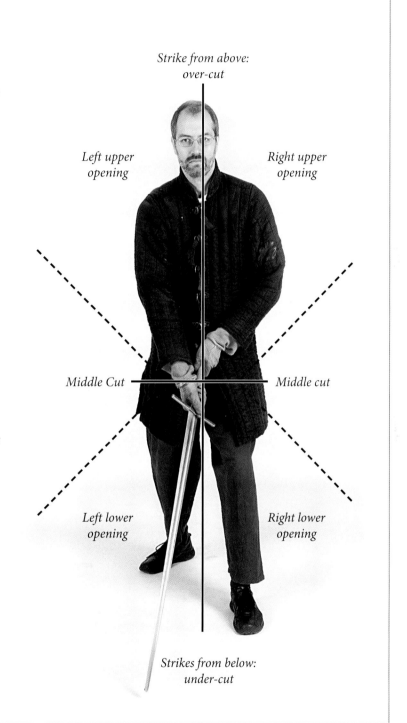

Strike from above:
over-cut

Left upper
opening

Right upper
opening

Middle Cut

Middle cut

Left lower
opening

Right lower
opening

Strikes from below:
under-cut

33

The Guards:
Beginning and End

A guard is a basic position. These guards are the starting point for most strikes and many strikes end in one of these guards. The Master Strikes (see next chapter) are executed from one guard to the other. Each guard thus forms a fixed point in combat, from which one continues fighting. They are positions from which we have a multitude of possibilities to continue fighting. Each guard also covers certain lines of attack. In combat it often happens that the opponents stand facing each other and, by changing guards, try to negate each others plans without delivering a blow.

Most guards, except the central ones, can be executed right or left. The terms right and left here refer to the position of the blade. If I stand with my left leg forward and have the blade on the right side, the guard is called right. If I stand with my right leg forward and the blade is on my left side, then I am making a left guard.

There are four basic guards in the German Liechtenauer school, the "Fool," "Plow," "Ox" and "Roof." Two other guards, the "Tail" and "Barrier," were added later. These six guards form the basis. There are other guards, such as the "Key," the "Iron Gate," the "Unicorn," the "Scales," etc. These additional guards were mentioned by some fencing masters, others ignored them completely. The six basic guards cover all possibilities, so that we will concentrate on them. Somewhat outside this list is the "Long Point," as it was mentioned and used by almost every fencing master but is usually not included in the list of guards.

THE FOOL (*Der Alber*):
This guard looks quite simple and also does not necessarily look threatening. This is a mistake, however, for one can fight very quickly and effectively from the Fool. The Fool is difficult to break. In the right Fool one stands with the left foot forward and holds the blade with the tip facing the ground. The blade is positioned centrally or points slightly to the outer right. The arms can be held near the body or extended. In the left Fool the right leg is forward, and the blade is on the left side with the tip on the ground. The long cutting edge faces the ground.

THE PLOW (*Der Pflug*):
The Plow is a guard which effectively covers either side. In the Plow we hold the hilt roughly at hip level. This points the tip at the opponent's face. In the left Plow the sword is held in the thumb grip, with the thumb lying on the surface of the blade. The sword is held in such a way that the wrists are straight. Especially in the left Plow, this means that the grip is somewhat turned in the hand. One can thrust very well from the Plow. Very quick, whip-like over cuts are also effective from the Plow. The Tick (more about this later) is especially successful from the Plow. The long edge faces downward in the right Plow, upwards in the left Plow.

THE OX (*Der Ochs*):
In the right Ox we again stand with the left leg forward. We raise the hilt high over and in front of the head. Generally the tip points slightly downward and toward the opponent. In both the left and right Ox we again use a thumb grip and place the thumbs on the bottom of the blade. This provides better stability. In the left Ox we stand with the right leg forward and hold the hilt on the left side. The arms are not crossed. The Ox threatens with the thrust. From the Ox one can also strike effectively with the Cross Strike (see next chapter). In the right Ox the long edge faces to the right, in the left Ox the short cutting edge faces left.

RIGHT FOOL

LEFT FOOL

RIGHT PLOW

LEFT PLOW

FROM THE ROOF (*vom Tag*):
Strictly speaking, there are three versions of the From the Roof: From the Roof (left and right), From the Roof on the Shoulder (left and right), and From the Roof over the Head (central). In all of the variants the blade points straight up or slightly to the rear. For the most part, strikes are made from the From the Roof Guard, thrusts very seldom.

In the From the Roof right, the hilt is held next to the right side of the head with the guard at eye level. In the From the Roof on the Shoulder, the blade rests on the shoulder and points slightly backward. The hilt rests comfortably just under the shoulder. In the From the Roof over the Head, the sword is raised centrally over the head and thus makes possible an attack from all sides.

In the From the Roof right and Over the Head, the long cutting edge faces forward, and to the rear in the From the Roof left. In the From the Roof on the Shoulder, the flat of the blade rests on the shoulder. Here the long cutting edge faces left outward. Be careful not to extend the forward elbow, otherwise it is an easy target. Instead, simply let it hang down.

TAIL GUARD (*Nebenhut*):
The Tail Guard is very simple. The blade points to the rear, the hilt is roughly at hip level. The Left Tail Guard, with the right leg forward, is executed with crossed hands. This guard is well-suited for under-cuts, but light over- or middle-cuts can also be struck from it. In the Tail Guard the long cutting edge faces forward. If the long cutting edge faces back, then one speaks of a Changer or Change Guard.

RIGHT OX

LEFT OX

RIGHT FROM
THE ROOF

FROM THE ROOF
ON THE SHOULDER

LEFT FROM
THE ROOF

FROM THE ROOF
OVERHEAD

BARRIER GUARD (*Schrankhut*):
The barrier guard forms a barrier in front of us. The sword is placed diagonally in front of us with the tip touching the ground. The hilt is above the knee of the front leg, the blade is on the side of the back leg. Crooked Strikes can be struck very well from this guard.

THE KEY (*Der Schlüssel*)
If, from the Ox, one allows the hilt to drop to shoulder height and takes it back, so that the blade rests on the forward upper arm, one is in the Key. Either the flat or edge of the blade can rest on the upper arm.

THE UNICORN (*Das Einhorn*):
The Unicorn is the final position after an under-cut. The tip points upward, and in a right Unicorn the arms are crossed.

HANGING GUARD (*Hangetort*):
The Hanging Guard is a guard in which the tip is suspended over the floor. If the right side is facing forward, then the tip points down to the left and vice versa.

THE LONG POINT (*Der Langort*):
In the Long Point the blade is stuck out straight in front of the body. Once again the tip points toward the opponent's face.

THE CHANGE (*Der Wechsel*):
The Change is actually the end position after a strike delivered downward from a high guard and is roughly similar to the Tail Guard. In the Change, the blade is to the right or left of the fighter, the long cutting edge facing towards the rear.

RIGHT TAIL GUARD

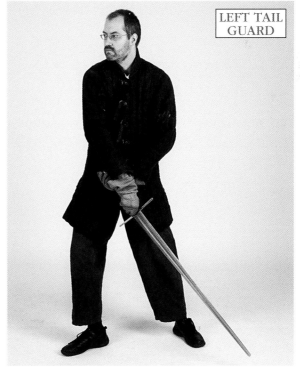

LEFT TAIL GUARD

RIGHT BARRIER GUARD

LEFT BARRIER GUARD

KEY

HANGING GUARD

LONG POINT

UNICORN

The Master Strikes:
High School of Fencing

In general, the master fencers summarized all blows struck from above as over-cuts and all blows struck from below as under-cuts. As well, there were also the five Master Strikes or Secret Strikes. These five Master Strikes are:

- Strike of Wrath (*Zornhau*)
- Crown Strike (*Scheitelhau*)
- Squinting Strike (*Schielhau*)
- Crosswise Strike (*Zwerchhau*)
- Crooked Strike (*Krumphau*)

In addition to the strike, almost all of the Master Strikes also cover an opponent's line of attack and so offer a cover at the same time as a strike. All Master Strikes have one thing in common: if a cut is made from the right, then the right leg also follows from back to front. An effort is always made to work from the body and not just with the arms. Incorporate hip movement and upper torso rotation into the blow and give it more power. In all Master Strike retain as upright a posture as possible.

The blade should always be guided as cleanly as possible. Try to guide the blade precisely on the cutting plane, without tilting the blade or deviating from the cutting plane. Use grip leverage to generate additional power: this can be achieved by pushing or pulling the pommel with your left hand. When possible, always strike at the enemy with the Master Strikes and not his weapon—there are exceptions, however, such as the Crooked Strike against the Long Point.

6.1 Strike of Wrath

The Strike of Wrath is the simplest but also the most important of the five Master Strikes. Special attention was paid to it in the fencing manuals. It is one of the most powerful and in terms of movement most natural strikes. It can be struck from the From the Roof, Plow, Ox and Tail Guards. Of course it is also possible from the Barrier and the Fool, but from these guards it takes more time and is rather predictable.

The Strike of Wrath is nothing more than a powerful cut from above from right to left. If one were to place a stick in the hand of a very angry man, he would probably strike a blow with it very similar to a Strike of Wrath.

For the right Strike of Wrath, we position ourselves in the right From the Roof Guard. Then we strike with the sword on a line from the starting position without drawing back, with the long cutting edge to the lower left facing downward. The right hand determines the direction of movement. The left hand uses the grip as a lever and thus moves the tip forward. The combination of the two moves ensures that the sword also cuts at the moment of impact. The strike is thus combined with a pulling cut. Meanwhile, we take a step forward with the right leg and thus bring the entire body movement into the blow. At the end we are standing in a position very similar to the left Plow.

Correspondingly, the left Strike of Wrath is made on the other side from above left to below right. Here, for example, one begins from the left From the Roof Guard and steps forward with the left leg. The final position is similar to the right Plow. The Strike of Wrath always ends in a lower hanging stance. Otherwise, it is a normal descending cut.

Strike of Wrath from the right: the fighters are standing in the From the Roof Guard.

While the hands execute the strike, the right leg moves forward.

When the blade makes contact, the right leg is on the ground and the stance is stable. The kinetic energy is transferred into the strike.

CHAPTER 6

The same motion sequence seen from the other side.

The blade leads the movement; body and leg follow.

Clean guidance of the blade is very important, so that the strike achieves its full effect.

VARIATIONS:

You can, of course, also execute the Strike of Wrath while moving back. Instead of stepping forward with the right leg, take a step back with the left leg. You execute the Strike of Wrath with no forward or backward movement simply with a change step (*Wechselschritt*).

An especially powerful Strike of Wrath is struck through, thus making it a normal descending cut. It is true that this blow is more powerful, but if one misses his opponent there is no longer any direct threat from the point, and one offers his counterpart a major opening for a counterattack. Because of the great momentum of the strike, it requires more time to parry the opponent's counter. Normally this descending cut ends in a Change Guard.

The Strike of Wrath also serves as the starting point for other Master Strikes. For example, one can begin with a Strike of Wrath, and then halfway through change it into a Crosswise, Squinting or Crooked Strike. This makes the Strike of Wrath unpredictable, and one can oneself react very well to the opponent's reactions. For this reason, the Strike of Wrath is ideally suited to the attack. It offers a vast array of possibilities.

There are also variations of the Strike of Wrath, which various fighters use in some situations. In the process, the boundary between over-cut and Strike of Wrath often becomes blurred. The most important variant is the "pushed Strike of Wrath." Begin in the Plow and push the blade forward without changing the thrust line. The blow is struck only at the last moment by pulling back the pommel. This Strike of Wrath is now very powerful, but it is very fast and difficult to judge. This form is also often used for the Tick.

It is important not to draw back and "announce" the strike.

The Strike of Wrath usually starts from a high guard—From the Roof, Plow or Ox.

It is tremendously important to bring the forward body movement and hip rotation into the strike.

Bring your blade forward without raising or lowering the point.

Do not strike until the end of the movement, by pulling the pommel upwards. Execute a pushing cut, and push your blade forward.

The Strike of Wrath end position: the Under Hang. This final position confirms that the stroke is combined with a pulled cut.

The final position after the blow has been struck through. This is considered an over-cut. This posture is also called Changer (Wechsler) or Change Guard (Wechselhut).

6.2 The Crown Strike

In practice, the Crown Strike is almost always struck from the From the Roof or Plow Guards. In the Crown Strike a vertical descending strike is made without endangering one's own hands. It is therefore preferred against the low guards such as the Fool, Barrier and Tail. The Crown Strike can be very useful in combat if one uses it to "strike over" a parry from above.

The Crown Strike can be executed from all of the guards from which the Strike of Wrath can also be struck. It is always made vertically from above to below, thus there are no left and right versions. You can also take a step forward or backward or simply remain standing.

NOTE:
The Crown Strike breaks the Fool Guard.

Begin in the From the Roof Guard. Now move the hands straight forward and up slightly. At the same time, make a downwards strike using grip leverage with the left hand. This draws the pommel to the right forearm. At the end, the point should be hanging in the direction of the opponent's face, and the hands should be over your head. If the opponent parries an over-cut with a Crown, the possibility often exists to still reach him with a clean Crown Strike.

The High Cut is effective against low guards or as a counter to an attack on the legs.

The blade is guided downwards in a straight line from over the head.

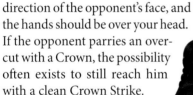

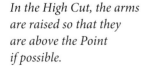

In the High Cut, the arms are raised so that they are above the Point if possible.

Once again the arms lead the way.

The High Cut from the other side.

The hands are raised, the point hangs down.
If the blow misses, you are in a thrusting position.

6.3 The Squinting Strike

The Squinting Strike rightly deserves to be called a Master Strike. It is not as simple to execute as the Strike of Wrath or Crown Strike, but properly employed it is tremendously effective. The Squinting Strike can be struck from all guards from which the Strike of Wrath can be executed. It combines two intentions in one strike: of course striking the enemy is the most important, but during the strike the opponent's blade is also deflected. This makes the Squinting Strike a "meanwhile" technique, for with it we can counter an opponent's attack and simultaneously attack him (more about this in Chapter 7). The Squinting Strike is therefore suitable for countering an attack, clearing a blade out of the way, creating an opening, or closing a line of attack. The series of movements that make up the Squinting Strike is quite complex. It can be executed from the Plow, From the Roof and Ox. The Squinting Strike is primarily used against "buffalos," fencers who rely on their power. It is used both against strikes and thrusts.

NOTE:
The Squinting Strike breaks the Plow Guard and the Long Point.

We begin the Squinting Strike from an upper guard, for example From the Roof on the Shoulder, followed by a normal Strike of Wrath until approximately the halfway point. Then we turn the blade with the short cutting edge forward and simultaneously guide it out to the left and forward. The hilt is out to the left just below shoulder height. During the turn we place the thumb on the blade for greater stability. We then strike the opponent's right shoulder with the short edge. At the same time, we take a step forward to the center. In the end position we are standing in a stable posture with the arms out to the left.

The short cutting edge has struck. If it did not strike, we are at least standing in a good thrusting position and should thrust immediately. The opponent's blade was deflected by our sideways movement, and we have stepped behind the opponent's thrust. It is important, if possible, to move the opponent's blade into a position of weakness or at least to the center. This means that we may need to raise our arms slightly.

The fighter (left) begins in From the Roof.

The Squinting Strike lands. If possible, your blade's forte should always be against the foible of the opponent's blade.

Here the Squinting Strike begins in the From the Roof on the Shoulder.

In the middle of the strike the blade is rotated outwards to the left, so that the thumb comes to lie on the flat and the long edge is pointing upwards.

In the end position push your blade out and left.
You may have to raise your hands to bind the foible of the opponent's blade.

6.4 The Cross Strike

The Cross Strike is a very ingenious strike, for it also enables us to manipulate the opponent's blade while we strike. As in the Squinting Strike, we can intercept the opponent's blade while it is moving, or bind and divert it in a guard. This also makes the Cross Strike a "meanwhile" technique. The Cross Strike breaks all of the opponent's descending cuts.

The Cross Strike can be executed from all guards from which the Strike of Wrath can be struck. When executing the Cross Strike, it is very important to step out of line, in order to, so to speak, stand beside the opponent. The farther we spring to the side, the easier it is to execute the Cross Strike. The more we remain in the center, the more force is required to move the opposing blade.

NOTE:
The Cross Strike breaks the From the Roof Guard.

We begin the Cross Strike, for example, from the right From the Roof Guard. We bring our hands forward and up, in front of and over our head. In doing so we turn our hands so that the short cutting edge faces forward and the blade is horizontal, placing our thumbs on the bottom of the blade. With this movement, our blade describes a semicircle on the horizontal plane with the short cutting edge forward. At the same time, we move our right leg outwards to the right and place our left leg in the basic position during the strike. We transfer the resulting rotation of the body to the blade and thus lend strength to the strike. The extended arms are important. The hilt covers the left side and upwards.

The Cross Strike: once again the fighter begins in From the Roof.

During the strike the blade is turned so that it is wielded horizontally with the short edge toward the opponent. Here the thumb rests on the underside of the flat. During the strike one steps or jumps to the outside.

The goal of the Cross Strike is to control the opponent's blade with your forte and strike the opening horizontally from the side.

Here the Cross Strike is begun from the From the Roof Guard on the shoulder.

The entire body rotation is transmitted to the blade, generating the required force.

In the end position of the Cross Strike it is important to be sure that the hilt is held above and in front of the head.

6.5 The Crooked Strike

The Crooked Strike is also a "meanwhile" technique. Here, however, the path of the opponent's blade is not changed as in the Crosswise and Squinting Strikes, rather one directly attacks the opponent's hands or blade. Only when attacking the opponent's hands can one speak of a meanwhile technique. As in the Cross Strike, in a Crooked Strike it is very important to jump out of line in time, in order to reach the correct position for the strike.

The Crooked Strike is suitable against all Crown Strikes and also low cuts. It can also be used very well against the Long point. The Crooked Strike can actually be struck from all guards.

NOTE:
The Crooked Strike breaks the Ox Guard and the Long point.

We begin the right Crooked Strike, for example, from the right Tail Guard. To reach the correct position, we jump forward diagonally on the right side. Simultaneously we guide the blade in front of our body like a windshield wiper from right below to left below. We strike with the long edge in the right Crooked Strike and the short edge in the left Crooked Strike. Once again we place the thumb on the flat of the blade. If we jump further forward then we can strike the opponent's hands, if we move more to the side, we can strike his blade. The Crooked Strike can also be struck diagonally forward if we need some range. When executing the Crooked Strike, one must be careful not to raise the hands too high.

The Crooked Strike: the fighter begins in the Tail Guard.

From the Tail Guard, the blade is moved forward in a circle in front of the body, with the long edge leading. The thumb is on the flat. In the process, one moves to the side and, depending on the measure, also slightly forward.

The Crooked Strike from the right strikes the opponent's blade with your blade's long edge.

Alternatively, one can also directly strike the opponent's arms with the Crooked Strike.

The Crooked Strike sequence from the front.

In the Crooked Strike, the blade is moved in a circular motion in front of the fighter like a windshield wiper.

Close-up of the point on the opponent's hands.

In the right Crooked Strike the long edge strikes.

The Five Words:
Timing and Technique

The German School is built upon four pillars: the three Wonders, the four Guards, the five Master Strikes and the five Words. These four pillars form the foundation of the German School. We have already met the wonders, guards, and Master Strikes. The Five Words are Before, Meanwhile, After, Weakness, and Strength.

Weak and Strong are terms for sections of the blade: the Strong, or Forte, is the back area of the blade, the Weak, or Foible, the front part (see drawing on Page 13). The understanding of Strong and Weak is enormously important. Only those who can handle this concept can fight well.

The terms Before, Meanwhile and After refer to the possible timings of every action. This refers to correct timing. One can achieve significantly more with little effort at the right time than with a great deal of effort at the wrong time. The concept of Before, Meanwhile and After is of great importance to sword fighting.

BEFORE (*Vor*):
Before characterizes basic actions taken prior to an attack by the opponent. The term "Before" can therefore be applied either to combat or to technique.

* Chronology in combat: in combat you should always try to be in the Before. That means you should strike the first blow or *Vorschlag* and continue to retain the initiative. The fighter in the Before acts, whereas the freighter in the After only reacts. If you fight in the Before, then you can apply your techniques and devices. You force your opponent to react to your attacks, and he will not be able to use his devices. As a result, in the end, you will defeat him.

* Chronology of a technique: if you want to break an opponent's technique, then you can best do it in the Before. That means that you make the break just as the opponent begins his technique, when it is nascent.

MEANWHILE (*Indes*):
Meanwhile means "simultaneously" or "at the same time." The Meanwhile is also used in combat and the various techniques. The old fencing masters believed: true masters fight in the "meanwhile" when possible.

* Chronology in combat: if you enter combat in the After, then you can get back to the Before by working Meanwhile. This means that you do not wait for the opponent's attack, instead you employ your device while the opponent is making his attack. Of course, this means that you must either avoid or parry his attack, while simultaneously yourself carrying out an attack with the same movement. Meanwhile techniques are suitable for this.

* Chronology of a technique: Meanwhile techniques are, for example, a Squinting or Cross Strike against a Crown Strike. In doing so, you break your opponent's attack and carry out an attack yourself with one and the same movement.

Illustration from Joachim Meyer's combat manual, 1600.

AFTER (*Nach*):

The term After essentially characterizes actions that are made in reaction to an attack by the opponent. After is always a reaction to Before. Here, too, there are two applications:

* Chronology in combat: as soon as you react to an attack by the opponent, you are in the After. That is to be avoided, for in After you can only react to attacks and cannot employ any of your own devices. Using Meanwhile techniques, you can go from the After to the Before. But you can also gain measure and once again try to attack from the Before.

* Chronology of a technique: techniques in the After work in reaction to a technique by the opponent. An example would be *Nachreisen im Nach*, in which you wait for an attack, evade it and then strike at the opening.

Keyword Measure: in combat the correct distance is as important as the correct timing, but in Liechtenauer's system the distance, or Measure, follows implicitly from his instructions. We have the moment of the action (for example Before), the means (for example Strike of Wrath), and the execution (for example strike) and the part of the blade with which we execute (for example the foible). The fencing master now says quite clearly that one should always strike the man and not his weapon. Thus the distance for this technique is settled: the correct distance is the one which, with the correct footwork for the technique (Strike of Wrath), causes the foible to strike the opponent.

55

Fundamental Techniques: Building Blocks of Combat

8.1 Cutting Off (*Abschneiden*)

Cutting with the sword is a very versatile and effective technique and the third of the three Wonders—striking, thrusting, cutting. The cut is often helpful in close quarters. It is used as a counter if the opponent tries to run in, as the start to your own running-in, or also to thwart an imminent attack by your opponent. Cutting Off (Abschneiden) can be executed with either a pulled or pushed cut. The pulled cut is more natural, as it usually continues the movement. The pushed cut closes the distance even further, and after a pushed cut you can usually easily begin wrestling (see Chapter 11). There are four different styles of slicing off—two high and two low.

In Cutting Off, it is important that you try to put your body weight into the step. Cutting Off generally means driving the opponent's arm away from his body. First and foremost, in the beginning phase of the cut you have the opponent's arms under control. At the end of the pulled cut you can usually make a thrust or strike, while a throw is possible at the end of a pushed cut.

THE FIRST AND THE SECOND CUT:
Your opponent tries to run in and overcome you from above left. Come under his arms with crossed arms and push his arms upwards and over him. If your opponent comes at you from above right, then take his arms with the short edge and force them upwards. Then you can begin wrestling, withdraw with another step, make a *Verkehrer* (see Chapter 8.10) or, depending on the opponent's position, employ other techniques.

THE THIRD CUT:
Both blades are in contact, the points pose no threat, and the direction of pressure is to the side. Your opponent pulls back his blade in order to strike you on the head from above. With hilt raised, slice through the arms from below and after the slice thrust into his chest. This is a break against the high withdrawal, but also a good technique if your opponent separates the blades by disengaging upwards.

THE FOURTH CUT:
If the opponent binds your sword from your left and shifts to your right side, striking with a Cross Strike or other technique, then step out of the way of the blow with your left leg and take him from above with your long edge over both arms. This works on both sides.

TRANSFORMATION OF THE CUTS:
On moving in, come under your opponent's arms with the long edge, your tip pointing toward your left side. Now push your opponent's arms to your right side, and slice around the arms with your long edge. Meanwhile push his arms away from you and down, so that in the end your sword comes to lie on top of the opponent's arms.

CUTTING OFF: FIRST AND SECOND CUTS

The fighters face each other in guard positions.

From the Bind, the female fighter tried to run in to begin wrestling.

The male fighter moves beneath her arms and forces them upward.

If the opponent approaches from the other side, move the short edge under his hands.

In withdrawing, the male fighter cuts across the arms of the female fighter.

You can also knock the opponent off balance by pushing on his elbows, before striking at an opening.

The opponent runs in from the left. Step 1	
ARMS:	Come under his hilt with your long edge, take his arms and push them upwards. Your cross guard keeps his arms from sliding down (Illustration 3)

The opponent runs in from the right. Step 1	
ARMS:	Your opponent comes from the right and begins wrestling.

Step 2:	
ARMS:	Your opponent runs in from the right. Come under his hilt with your short edge, take his arms and push them upwards.
LEGS:	Step slightly to the right with your front leg. All subsequent steps then result from the measure, the opponent's reaction and your pursuing technique.

CUTTING OFF: THIRD CUT

1

The third cut. You are in a Bind.

Step 1:

ARMS: You are in a Bind. Your opponent raises his arms. Immediately come under his arms with your long edge. It is important that you do not hesitate. As soon as your opponent raises his arms, lay your long edge on his arms.

BODY: Be sure to keep your body upright. Do not bend in order to get under his arms. You generate the necessary force from your upright body. It is sufficient if you lean forward slightly.

LEGS: Depending on the measure, take a step forward. Whether you do this with the front or back leg depends on the distance you have to cover. In this technique it is important to step out of line to the right.

Step 2:

ARMS: Move your blade close, then push the opponent's arms upwards. From this position thrust at his chest.

Your opponent raises his arms, to free himself from the bind upwards. You come under his arms, cut…

… and then thrust into his chest while withdrawing.

CUTTING OFF: FOURTH CUT

1

The fourth cut. The female fighter attempts to pull away to strike a blow on the other side.

2

As she does this, the male fighter falls on her hands.

Step 1	
ARMS:	You are in a Bind. Your opponent now pulls away to strike a blow on the other side. Strike his arms from above with your long edge. It is important that you gain control of his arms, so that his blow does not land.
LEGS:	Be sure to keep your body upright. Do not bend in order to get under his arms. You generate the necessary force from your upright body. It is sufficient if you lean forward slightly.

CUTTING OFF: TRANSFORMATION OF THE CUTS

1

The male fighter comes under the arms with his long edge. His point is pointing to his left side.

2

The male fighter cuts around the female fighter's arms in a fluid motion, forcing her arms to the side and down.

Step 1	
ARMS:	During combat slice the opponent's arms from below with your long edge (for example from the Crown). Force his arms upwards and slice.

Step 2	
ARMS:	You now push his arms to the right and bring your sword over his arms, so that your long edge comes to rest on top of his arms. You can also thrust from this position.

8.2 Setting Aside (*Das Absetzen*)

Setting Aside is a very important technique. It is one of the Meanwhile techniques and as such is very effective. The objective of Setting Aside is to deflect the opponent's blade and aim one's own point at the opponent. The opponent's forward movement during the attack causes him to run toward the point. If one also moves forward during the Setting Aside, then the impact is very hard and the thrust very deep. In training, this technique often leads to the fighter literally being hurled backwards. With Setting Aside, one can parry every over- or under-cut and most thrusts. This technique is therefore very often employable.

Setting Aside does, however, illustrate an important basic posture in sword fighting: always try to receive the threat with the point raised. If you are unable to attack from the Setting Aside, then you are automatically a danger because of the forward-pointing tip. You force the opponent to first deal with this threat before he can bring his own techniques to bear. Through the Meanwhile technique of Setting Aside, therefore, you have gone from the After to the Before and now have the initiative in the combat.

There are four setting aside techniques: two high (left and right) and two low (left and right). In their postures they resemble the Ox and Plow Guards, each left and right. In the Setting Aside it is important to turn one's blade towards the opponent's blade so that the opponent's blade is intercepted by the cross guard and simultaneously forced outwards.

EXAMPLE 1: The attacker begins the combat with a Strike of Wrath. The defender moves up and to the left out of the Plow and catches the attacker's blade, while he aims his point at the attacker's face. In doing so he takes a step forward. This deflects the attacker's blade and the thrust lands.

SETTING ASIDE AGAINST AN OVER-CUT

Setting Aside against an over-cut. Here you see well how the male fighter closes the female fighter's line of attack.

Step 1

ARMS: From The Roof, move your arms up and to the left, so that your hilt ends up over and above your head. It is important to position your blade so that it catches the opponent's blade. The point hangs to the middle, towards the opponent's head or chest. This forms a wedge that forces away the opponent's blade. You may also want to use the thumb grip for this technique.

BODY: Turn into the thrust with your body, so that you can reliably intercept a powerful Strike of Wrath. Make sure to keep your body upright.

LEGS: Depending on the measure, step forward, backward or to the side with a change step. If possible step forward, so as to give your thrust more power and range. By stepping forward, you also take the opponent's blade reliably with your cross guard.

ADDITIONAL EXAMPLES OF SETTING ASIDE

The female fighter attacks with a Strike of Wrath.

The defender positions his blade with a forward thrust and turns away the opponent's blade. This is an example of setting aside a Strike of Wrath.

Setting Aside against an under-cut: this technique demands special care, for depending on the slope of your own blade and the opponent's striking plane, the blades may be almost parallel. Here you must pay attention to the necessary binding of the blades.

EXAMPLE 2: The attacker makes an under-cut, which the defender parries from the Plow position. The defender takes a step forward and thus strikes the attacker.

8.3 Setting Upon

Setting Upon, or *Ansetzen*, is a technical term for a thrust. The technique characterized as Setting Upon is actually following the opponent's movement in the Before (see 8.4). The objective here is to follow the opponent's drawing back movement with a thrust. As the opponent draws back to strike, we thrust into his opening.

Of course, Setting Upon can also be used when changing guards. If you are standing close enough, Setting Upon can be used, for example if the opponent changes from The Fool to From the Roof. Setting Upon only works if you are in a close measure. It is absolutely necessary that you can reach the opponent with the thrust without taking more than a half-step. Setting Upon can be executed from any guard, but preferably from the Plow, Ox or Fool.

The Setting Upon technique also clearly shows why one shouldn't draw back to strike a blow: not only does one prematurely betray his intention to the opponent, one also leaves an opening which can easily be attacked with the Setting Upon technique.

THE LOW SETTING UPON

The fighters face each other in their guards.

The female fighter draws back to make a thrust and pulls her sword back. The male fighter follows up immediately and thrusts into the opening.

Step 1	
ARMS:	The opponent draws his arms and weapon back, to reach back or change a guard. Thrust straight forward into the resulting opening.
BODY:	As always in a thrust, try to generate more power by leaning forward with the body.
LEGS:	No steps are taken during Setting Upon. If you cannot reach the opponent with half a step, then you should not attempt Setting Upon.

SETTING UPON WHILE REACHING BACK

The fighters are in guards.

If one fighter draws back his weapon in a reaching-back movement, the other fighter thrusts into the resulting opening. Here the reaching back movement is made upwards, therefore the thrust is directed against the upper opening.

If the opponent draws his blade back and down, follow up into the lower opening.

SETTING UPON WHILE CHANGING GUARDS

Setting Upon during a change of guard. Here the fighter changes from a Fool to From the Roof.

The female fighter attacks as her opponent is moving to change guards.

8.4 Chasing

Chasing, or *Nachreisen*, is based on a simple principle: each attack simultaneously leaves an opening. Chasing simply means attacking the unguarded spots resulting from an opponent's blow. There are three different versions of Chasing: Chasing in the Before, Meanwhile and After.

CHASING IN THE BEFORE
The objective of Chasing in the Before is to attack the opponent's openings before he can carry out his attack. The best example of this is if your opponent draws back for a blow. During this drawing back motion, you simply thrust into the resulting opening. This is also one reason why all blows should be struck seamlessly without drawing back.

CHASING IN THE MEANWHILE
When Chasing in the Meanwhile, you avoid the opponent's blade and strike at the opponent at the same time. An example of this is Over-Running. If you do not evade, then you must bind the opponent's blade and work over the opposing blade. An example of this would be the Cross Strike against an over-cut.

CHASING IN THE AFTER
Every blow, every attack, reveals an opening on the attacker. You exploit this fact in the Chasing in the After technique, in that you wait for his attack and, after avoiding his blade, attack this opening.

Example: Your opponent attacks with a Strike of Wrath. You evade by stepping straight back far enough to cause the blow to miss. Now you immediately strike in the upper opening. If the opponent parries your blade by raising his sword, strike his blade powerfully and slice over his arms or through his face.

If you chase and the enemy deflects your blow and forces your blade upwards, then go to his blade's foible and thrust into available openings (mutate).

CHASING IN THE AFTER

The fighters face each other in their guards.

The female attacker begins with a middle cut. The defender steps back to avoid the blow.

The defender strikes behind the attacker's blade into the opening.

CHASING IN THE AFTER

The fighters face each other in their guards.

The female fighter attacks with a Strike of Wrath. The defender steps back slightly to allow the attacker's blade to pass.

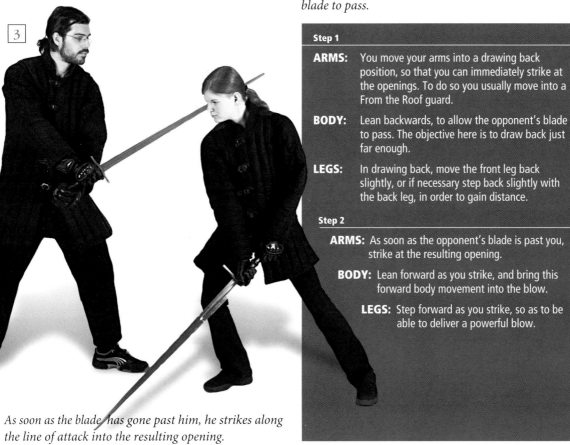

As soon as the blade has gone past him, he strikes along the line of attack into the resulting opening.

Step 1

ARMS: You move your arms into a drawing back position, so that you can immediately strike at the openings. To do so you usually move into a From the Roof guard.

BODY: Lean backwards, to allow the opponent's blade to pass. The objective here is to draw back just far enough.

LEGS: In drawing back, move the front leg back slightly, or if necessary step back slightly with the back leg, in order to gain distance.

Step 2

ARMS: As soon as the opponent's blade is past you, strike at the resulting opening.

BODY: Lean forward as you strike, and bring this forward body movement into the blow.

LEGS: Step forward as you strike, so as to be able to deliver a powerful blow.

8.5 Running Through

Running Through, or *Durchlaufen*, characterizes a closing technique in which one holds the sword in one hand with the blade hanging over one's back and runs through beneath one's own blade. One is guarded by the blade on one's back. The running through technique is usually followed by throw techniques. Running through can be used from a blade against blade position, but also as a response to an over-cut. In a bind position, usually the Crown or a high bind, one holds the sword with the left hand on the pommel and lets it hang over the back. Then one steps behind the opponent's left leg with his right and grasps the opponent around the body. In this way one throws the opponent to the ground in front of one.

The Running Through technique can also be executed by placing the right leg in front of the opponent's right leg, ducking under his right arm, grasping him from behind and throwing him backwards over the hip. The Running Through technique can also be executed on the other side. In this case you grab the opponent with the left hand and hold the sword in the right.

RUNNING THROUGH

1

The fighters are in a high bind, blade against blade. They are in a strong bind.

Variant 1	
Throw to the Rear from Running Through	
ARMS:	In the Bind, let go of your sword with your right hand and raise your left arm with the sword. Step through under your left arm, so that your sword now hangs over your back. With your right arm, simultaneously reach from in front around your opponent's chest and pull him down to the left over your hip.
BODY:	Be sure that your hip is directly against your opponent's body. The closer you are to the opponent's body, the easier will your throw succeed. Throw your opponent over your right hip with a turning movement. Keep your body's center of gravity lower than that of your opponent.
LEGS:	While Running Through, step your right leg behind the right leg of your opponent. This places your hip against the opponent and deprives him of the ability to step backwards.

Variant 2	
Forward Throw from Running Through	
ARMS:	In the Bind, again let go of your sword with your right hand, run through and with your right arm reach around your opponent's ribcage from behind.
BODY:	Here once again, be sure that your hip is against the opponent's body. The more upright your body is, the easier will the throw succeed. Be sure that your body's center of gravity is lower than that of your opponent.
LEGS:	While Running Through, step your right leg in front of your opponent's legs, so that your hip is against his body. During the throw, possibly step forward with your left leg in order to get more momentum into the throw.

2a

The fighter now lets his blade hang over his back and grasps the opponent around the breast.

2b

From the Crown, the fighter now grabs his opponent from behind around the ribcage.

3a

With a turning movement he throws his opponent forward over his hip.

3b

With a turning movement he throws his opponent behind him.

8.6 Changing Through

Changing Through, or *Durchwechseln*, is a very important and versatile technique. Its objective is always to leave the attack path and to work toward the opposing openings. This is achieved by dropping the point beneath the opponent's blade and thrusting to the other side. The opponent tries to bind your blade, and by missing leaves himself vulnerable. Put simply, the Changing Through technique is nothing more than an attack, usually a thrust, to the opposite side of where you are currently standing. The Changing Through technique is a variation of a *Fehler* (see 8.8).

The Changing Through technique is particularly effective against a fighter who seeks to bind and always wants to deflect the opponent's blade, one who relies very heavily on blocks and parries.

The Changing Through technique can be executed with or without blade contact. Be sure that the opponent's thrust is not aimed directly at you. In this case, under no circumstances should you change through, for otherwise you will easily run into the opponent's blade. Obviously, the opponent's point should also not pose a direct threat.

Example: the attacker begins with an over-cut. The defender responds with a Strike of Wrath and seeks to bind blade against blade. The attacker now lets his point drop under the defender's blade and thrusts at an opening from the other side, stepping to the side in the process. The thrust usually takes place from the hanging position.

Changing Through can be both an offensive and a defensive technique. If you are attacking, then you can change through if the opponent tries to deflect your attack. If you are the defender and are fighting in the After, then you can change through under the opponent's attack or change through out of the resulting bind. In this way you get out of the After and back into Before.

CHANGING THROUGH FROM THE BIND

The fighters face each other in their guards.

Again they strike Strike of Wrath against Strike of Wrath.

The attacker lets his point drop and dives through under the female fighter's blade, while pulling his hilt upwards.

After the attacker has avoided the blade of his opponent, he thrusts into the opening from the other side. If possible, one should always thrust from an Ox position.

Step 1	
ARMS:	You make an over-cut at the opponent. This must be as threatening as possible, for otherwise the opponent will not react to it. As soon as the opponent tries to parry your over-cut, change through.
Step 2	
ARMS:	As you move, allow your point to drop, and raise your hands with the hilt. In doing so, you guide your point through, under the opponent's blade.
BODY:	While diving through, you can go into the Crouch, in order to be better able to avoid the opponent's blade.
Step 3	
ARMS:	Raise your hands again, and thrust from the high hanging point into the opponent's opening.
LEGS:	As you dive through with the point toward the other side, step forward diagonally to the left out of line. Whether you are attacking or reacting to the opponent's attack, step out of line with your left or right leg.

CHANGING THROUGH FROM THE LONG POINT

The attacker binds in the Long Point.

The defender changes through on the left side and thrusts into the opening.

Step 1	
ARMS:	You are standing in the Long Guard. Your opponent tries to bind your blade with a Crooked or Squinting Strike.
Step 2:	
ARMS:	At best, just before the blades bind, change through to the other side. A small semicircular motion with your point, which you make with the wrist, is sufficient.
Step 3:	
ARMS:	You now continue the movement without interruption and thrust into the open opening.
LEGS:	Here you taker a half step forward and to the left side, in order for the thrust to have enough force and to achieve a close measure.

8.7 Drawing

Drawing, or *Das Zucken*, is a type of Changing Through. In contrast to the Changing Through technique, in Drawing one does not "dive through" under the opponent's blade, instead one's own blade is simply drawn back to allow the opposing blade to pass. This is immediately followed by another thrust. Drawing is used when our foible is against the opponent's forte. From the description it is apparent that the direction of pressure of the opposing blade should be to the side. Obviously the opposing blade should be upright enough so that it doesn't strike us if we refuse to bind. Optimally, one also steps left out of line when Drawing. The blades are often separated by this sideways movement and one can thrust directly.

Of course one can also use the Drawing technique to avoid binding blades. Drawing is often successful, especially when one attacks with a Strike of Wrath. When you attack with a Strike of Wrath, your opponent may seek to bind. Deny him this bind by drawing just before the blades touch and thrusting to the other side.

DRAWING FROM THE BIND

The fighters face each other in their guards.

Again an attack with a Strike of Wrath is countered with a Strike of Wrath. In the Bind the attacker's |foible is on the defender's forte.

The attacker draws his blade straight back and disengages the Bind.

Then he thrusts straight forward into the resulting opening.

Step 1	
ARMS:	From the Bind, pull your arms straight back to disengage the Bind. Pay attention to your opponent's direction of pressure in the Bind. If he is pressing straight towards you, then do not draw.
BODY:	The body should be upright.
LEGS:	Step to the left out of the line. Depending on the situation, that can be done with a half-step or a whole step. In the process pay attention to your balance.

Step 2	
ARMS:	Immediately after the Bind is disengaged, thrust straight forward on the other side. Depending on the situation, you can also try to cover the line.
BODY:	During the thrust it is often necessary to move the body forward for increased range.
LEGS:	With a small half-step you may also allow yourself to "fall" into the thrust.

DRAWING WITH NO BIND

Drawing with no blade contact: the fighters strike into the Bind.

Shortly before the Bind the attacker pulls back his blade …

… and thrusts into the opening that has been created.

8.8 Feints (*Fehler*)

Of course there are also feints and deceptive maneuvers in historical sword fighting. They are characterized as *Fehler*. In the *Fehler*, an attack provokes the opponent to move his blade, which is followed by an attack on the resulting openings. Naturally the *Fehler* is particularly suited for use against fighters who are fond of setting opponents' blades aside. The *Fehler* is therefore not a suitable technique for beginning a combat, as the opponent's reactions cannot yet be judged.

Anyone who initiates a *Fehler* of course runs the risk of being struck if the opponent does not react to the feint. It is thus always a gamble. The first attack must therefore be as convincing as possible, to be sure that the opponent reacts to it. If he fails to react, then the first attack is simply carried through to the end. Several examples for such maneuvers follow, without however making any claims to completeness.

CHANGING THROUGH FROM THE CROOKED STRIKE

The attacker makes an over-cut. The defender begins with a Crooked Strike, but intentionally strikes it too short, passes his point under the attacker's blade and thrusts into an opening from the other side. It is important to hold the hilt high to cover the head.

FEHLER WITH THE CROSSWISE CUT TO PLOW

The attacker approaches the defender. The attacker then feigns an over-cut or Strike of Wrath. As soon as the defender reacts, the attacker strikes a Cross Strike to Plow, directed against the lower openings. It is important that the attacker not strike two blows, instead changing his Strike of Wrath into a hanging Cross Strike during the movement.

THE FEHLER FROM THE CROOKED STRIKE

The fighters face each other in their guards. The female fighter feigns a Crooked Strike, which the male fighter tries to deflect. But she dives through under his blade...

... and thrusts to the other opening.

Step 1:		
ARMS:	You begin a Crooked Strike but do not strike him on the side; instead, you strike him too short directly in front of you.	
LEGS:	Do not step too far to the side. Instead remain on line.	

Step 2:		
ARMS:	As soon as you see that the opponent is reacting to your Crooked Strike, dive through under his blade with your point and thrust into his vulnerable spot from the other side.	
BODY:	Here "wind" your body into the correct thrusting position.	
LEGS:	Depending on stance and measure, you may have to execute one or other correcting steps.	

THE FEHLER WITH CROSS STRIKE FROM THE PLOW

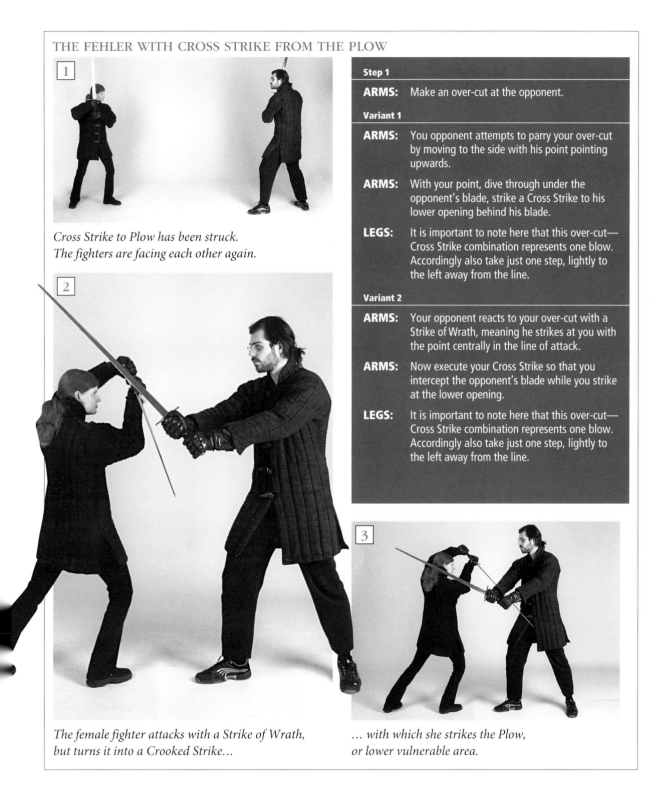

*Cross Strike to Plow has been struck.
The fighters are facing each other again.*

Step 1	
ARMS:	Make an over-cut at the opponent.
Variant 1	
ARMS:	You opponent attempts to parry your over-cut by moving to the side with his point pointing upwards.
ARMS:	With your point, dive through under the opponent's blade, strike a Cross Strike to his lower opening behind his blade.
LEGS:	It is important to note here that this over-cut—Cross Strike combination represents one blow. Accordingly also take just one step, lightly to the left away from the line.
Variant 2	
ARMS:	Your opponent reacts to your over-cut with a Strike of Wrath, meaning he strikes at you with the point centrally in the line of attack.
ARMS:	Now execute your Cross Strike so that you intercept the opponent's blade while you strike at the lower opening.
LEGS:	It is important to note here that this over-cut—Cross Strike combination represents one blow. Accordingly also take just one step, lightly to the left away from the line.

The female fighter attacks with a Strike of Wrath, but turns it into a Crooked Strike…

… with which she strikes the Plow, or lower vulnerable area.

THE DOUBLE FEHLER

The attacker approaches and makes as if about to strike a right Cross Strike. The Cross Strike is then "twitched," meaning struck short, and the attacker strikes the defender on the right side of his head. The blade remains as it is, meaning that the long edge is used. If he deflects this, the attacker aims another Cross Strike at the defender's right side, subsequently winds his sword with the short edge on the defender's sword, and cuts through the defender's face with the long edge. Alternately, at the end one can also fall upon the opponent's hands and slice them.

Variant 1: One can also execute this double Fehler from an over-cut: "twitch" it and then work as usual.

Variant 2: There are also differing interpretations. One of them is that after "twitching" the first Cross Strike, another Cross Strike is struck on the defender's right side. Personally, however, I prefer the first variant, as it appears to me to be faster.

THE DOUBLE FEHLER

1

The female attacker begins with a right Cross Strike.

Step 1	
ARMS:	Strike at the opponent with a Cross Strike. Be sure that you keep the Cross Strike under control.
BODY:	Good balance is a basic requirement of this technique.
LEGS:	Do not step too far to the side, instead stay on the line of attack.

Step 2	
ARMS:	As soon as your opponent reacts to the Cross Strike and tries to parry, pull your blade back and strike at the right side of his head with the short edge. This takes some practice.
BODY:	Generate the force for the blow to the head with the grip and, in particular, by rotating the hips slightly.

Step 3	
ARMS:	If he parries this blow, then strike at the same side of the head again with another Cross Strike.
LEGS:	Here you make a change step on the spot. Do not step closer to the opponent when you make the second Cross Strike.

Step 4	
ARMS:	If he also parries this blow, then take the short edge of the opponent's blade with the short edge of your blade and slice through his face with a pushing slice. In doing so you can push his blade against his body with your cross guard.
LEGS:	Depending on the measure, you can take a step here.

Step 5	
ARMS:	As you withdraw, cut him with your long edge over his shoulder and/or hands.
LEGS:	Depending on the measure, you can take a step here.

The defender attempts to parry it.

The female fighter then twitches her Cross Strike.

She strikes at the head from the other side.

CHAPTER 8

If the fighter also parries this blow …

… then the female fighter strikes a left Cross Strike …

… doubles behind the opponent's blade …

… places her long edge on his head …

… and slices through his face.

8.9 Overrunning

If the opponent attacks the lower openings, then instead of parrying it you should instead simply strike his head. This is called Overrunning, or *Überläufen*. The distance from your opponent to your legs is longer than the distance from you to his head. It is thus possible to strike the opponent's head from a safe distance, without being struck in the legs.

This of course applies to all attacks that are struck directly towards your lower openings. Here you always have a range advantage with a Crown Strike. Overrunning explains why the legs are almost never considered a target.

OVERRUNNING

The fighters face each other in their guards.

The female attacker begins by striking at the defender's front leg. He pulls his leg back and in doing so makes a Crown Strike.

Step 1	
ARMS:	Your opponent strikes at your legs. That can happen from a variety of situations.
Step 2	
ARMS:	Strike at the opponent's head with a Crown Strike. Be sure to extend your arms.
BODY:	Be sure to maintain an absolutely upright posture.
LEGS:	Withdraw the front leg so that it cannot be struck. You are then standing with both legs together or have taken a step back.

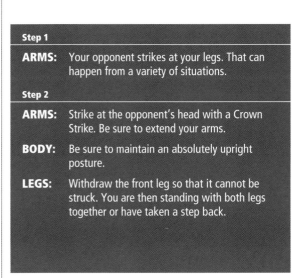

Because of the longer range, the defender's blow lands, while the female attacker misses.

8.10 The Verkehrer

Basically the *Verkehrer* technique uses the power of the opponent. If your opponent thrusts in a particular direction, then you yield in that direction and push his arm in the same direction at the elbow. By pushing on the elbow, you have good leverage, and your opponent has already directed his power in the direction of the thrust. In this way, it is often possible that your opponent will fall to the ground when the *Verkehrer* is employed. At the very least, he will almost certainly lose his balance.

Example: If you bind the opponent's sword with an over- or under-cut, then turn your sword so that your thumb comes to rest on the bottom of the blade and thrust it from above at the opponent's face. This forces him to deflect the thrust. If he does deflect the thrust, then grab the opponent's right elbow with your left hand, step your left leg in front of his right leg and then throw him. Or run through and wrestle.

The *Verkehrer* can also be used effectively if your opponent parries in the Crown. You then simply push him backwards by his elbows. Take care to confirm that you push the opponent's left elbow over his right shoulder and vice versa.

THE VERKEHRER

The fighters face each other in their guards.

They come into Bind …

… and the fighter on the right thrusts at the face.

The fighter on the left parries this thrust, …

… whereupon the fighter on the right steps in front of the other fighter's leg, grabs his elbow …

… and pushes him forward by the elbow or throws him.

Step 1		
ARMS:		From the Bind you force the opponent to parry aggressively. This can be done very easily with a thrust to the face. Hold your sword so that your thumb comes to rest on the bottom of the blade.

Step 2		
ARMS:		If your opponent parries this thrust, then release the grip with your left hand and grab the opponent's right elbow. If your opponent now deflects your blade out to the right, then push him in that direction. If he deflects your blade upwards, then push him up and back. In other words, follow his direction of pressure.
BODY:		Be sure to maintain an upright posture.
LEGS:		Here you should already step in front of his legs. You reduce the measure, in order to be able to grab his elbow, and you prevent your opponent from taking a step to regain his balance.

Step 3		
ARMS:		Either cause him to fall or strike at the now available opening.
LEGS:		Either step in front of his legs (if pushing sideways) or behind his legs (if pushing backwards).

79

THE VERKEHRER FROM THE CROWN

The Verkehrer also works from the Crown. Your opponent makes a strong Bind.

Grab his elbow with your left hand and push him backwards.

End the play with a pommel strike, for example.

8.11 The Tick (*Das Zecken*)

The Tick is a very fast technique which is mainly used to wear down the opponent. In particular, the Tick can be used at the beginning of a combat as the fighters approach. While you will not be able to decide a combat in your favor with certainty with the Tick, with it you will put the opponent off his stride or see to it that he is no longer able to use one hand.

Short, quick strikes with the point on the hands or forearms are characterized as Ticks. One uses the maximum range, rushes forward, and strikes the arm with the point.

Ticking is very nerve-wracking and difficult to prevent, especially for unpracticed fighters. But don't underestimate the weight and power of the Tick! By precisely controlling the blade you can inflict serious damage.

THE TICK

The fighter on the left is standing in a From the Roof guard but sticks his elbow out too far.

The fighter on the right immediately strikes at his elbow.

Step 1

ARMS: You strike forward with your sword in a fast, whipping movement and strike the forearm or hands with the point. It is important to execute the Tick with no drawing back movement. The faster the blow comes, the better. In the Tick you only strike with the point.

BODY: If necessary stretch forward to momentarily gain increased range. But be sure that you do not lean so far forward that you cannot instantly pull back again should the enemy initiate an attack.

LEGS: The Tick is usually executed with no footwork. After the Tick you should immediately hurry back, in order to give the opponent no opportunity for an attack. This only works if no additional footwork is necessary.

Winding:
Combat Blade on Blade

Winding, or *Das Winden*, is a central technique in the German School. Winding is understood to mean work with the blades bound, in which one attempts to work one's way toward the opponent's openings while, if possible, retaining blade contact.

There are a total of 24 Winds. Harald Winter von Dreynschlag wrote:

> *"**ONE** Wind in*
> *   **TWO** directions with the*
> *   **THREE** wonders to the*
> *   **FOUR** openings."*

One can also wind to all four outer and inner openings with the three Wonders. Two times three times four makes twenty-four. As soon as the blades are in contact, you have the opportunity to bind. Winding should be executed as quickly as possible, forcefully and especially in a winding forward movement.

9.1 Two Directions: Inner and Outer

If you are standing in bind, seen from your position you have an inner and an outer side. If you strike a right over-cut and end up in a Bind, then your left side is your inner side and your right side is your outer side. The sides are reversed in a left over-cut.

If the pressure is not too great, then you can wind inwards. If the outward pressure, to the side, is very great, however, then it is better to wind outward, for the pressure of the opponent's blade will confirm that the bind is maintained. If you wind inward after a right over-cut, then you guide your hilt up and to the left, toward your opponent's right opening.

9.2 Winding with the Three Wonders

If you are standing at a medium measure, then you can thrust well from a Wind; if you are standing closer, then you Wind into a blow. If you are at close distance, then you Wind the blade onto the opponent's neck, for example, and make a pushing or pulling slice.

The Wind is executed somewhat differently depending on the distance from the opponent, pressure, blade position, bind and opponent. In the following, therefore, I will explain just one style of Winding. All of the other possibilities can be derived from it, however. The only important thing in Winding is that it be carried out as forcefully as possible and with a forward-directed movement. The object is to have the opponent's blade under control while working directly towards the openings.

9.3 Practical Use

We assume the following opening situation in our practical example: both fighters have struck a right over-cut and ended up in a binding position. The pressure is equally distributed, and both fighters are equally strong in the bind. They then raise their arms over their heads to the left and extend them. As a result of this movement, you take the foible of the opponent's blade with the short edge of your forte and simultaneously push it out of the way. Meanwhile you aim your point in the direction of the opponent's face and thrust.

WINDING FROM THE BIND

The fighters are in a bind.

The male fighter winds inside and upwards and thrusts into the opening.

Step 1

ARMS: Remain in the bind and, in a rotating motion, raise your hilt out and to the left. Your short edge is now on the opponent's blade. Your thumb is on the bottom of the flat, your hands and your hilt are above and to the left of your head. This rotating motion is now carried out to the front, so that the rotation becomes a sort of screwing movement. In other words, you thrust aggressively into the opponent while gaining control of his blade.

BODY: Lean forward as you thrust, and also bring your hips into the forward screwing movement, in order to lend more force to the action.

LEGS: If you are not standing close enough, then take a half-step forward with your front leg. Calmly let yourself fall into this step somewhat, in order to give the Winding movement more power and momentum.

He can also bring the blade into contact …

… and slice.

83

The fighters are in a bind. The female fighter on the right is in a strong bind and pushing to the side.

The fighter on the left therefore winds upwards and from the outside toward the opening.

If your opponent is very strong in the bind, however, then Wind outwards. To do this you raise your arms over your head to the right and take the short edge of your opponent's blade with your hilt and thrust over his sword to his face.

Another technique from the Wind: you are standing in a bind and Wind up and to the left. If the opponent pushes hard against this, then strike behind his sword with the short edge to his neck. Of course, in this situation you can also try to Wind to the outside. What action you take depends in part on your opponent's direction of pressure.

9.4 Mutation (*Mutieren*)

The Mutation is a continuation or part of the Wind. Mutating describes a change in the attack: for example, from cut to thrust, or a change in the attacked opening. For this reason there are many types of Mutation. I would like to describe just one form here.

In Winding, it often happens that your opponent deflects your thrust by raising his hilt, thus going into a Crown. In this situation, you go to his foible and push his blade downward, while thrusting around his arms to the lower opening. Here the Mutation is nothing more than taking the opposing blade while thrusting to another opening. One changes the target and simply takes the opposing blade along. Of course the Mutation can be used in any situation in which you can safely take the foible of the opposing blade before working your way toward the opening.

MUTATION

1

The fighters are facing each other.

2

In the Bind, the fighter on the right takes the initiative…

3

… and takes the foible of the opponent's blade.

4

Through the foible he controls the opponent's blade and thrusts outside past the arms to the lower opening.

5

In the Mutation, from the Bind one thrusts from the outside to the lower opening.

Step 1	
ARMS:	You have tried to wind in a high thrust, and your opponent has parried this with the Crown, moving his hilt upwards. Now you take his foible with your forte and bring your point downward. This also works without the previous Winding. You simply Mutate immediately.
Step 2	
ARMS:	Now push his blade to the side, while you thrust past his arms to the lower opening.
LEGS:	If the measure requires, take a step forward with your left leg.

9.5 The Doubling (*Duplieren*)

The Doubling is a fast technique which can almost never be broken. It does, however, demand a very good reaction from the fighter executing it. In principle the Doubling is actually a Wind. In the Doubling two strikes are made from one—the strike is therefore doubled.

You are standing in a bind, and your opponent is hard in the bind, blade on blade, the direction of pressure more to the side. This is the optimal situation for the Doubling technique. In Doubling the blades remain in the bind, but you strike behind the opponent's blade to his head. As a result, your blade ends up between the opponent and his blade.

Should your opponent be quick enough, then he can break the Doubling by raising his hilt into a Crown position. In this improbable event, stay on his blade and Mutate to his lower opening. This means that you push his foible aside and thrust to his lower opening. At that point, however, you can also very effectively employ a *Verkehrer* or begin wrestling.

THE DOUBLING

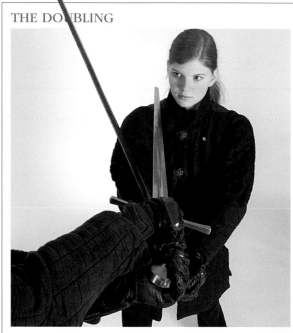

In the Doubling, strike at the opponent's head behind his blade.

Step 1	
ARMS:	Stay in the Bind, and move your pommel to the right, beneath your right elbow. This moves your point to the left side. Your blade is now between the opponent's blade and his head.
Step 2	
ARMS:	Now strike behind his blade directly at his head with your long edge.
LEGS:	Here perhaps take a step forward and slightly to the side with your left leg, in order to give the blow more force.
Variants:	
ARMS:	You can also strike the opponent's head from the outside with the short edge of the blade. While in the bind, you strike his head with the short edge from the right in a flowing movement. Here, too, you again guide your pommel through under your right arm.

The fighters are in the bind, forte on forte; the female fighter's direction of pressure is to the side. She is in a rather strong bind.

The fighter now Doubles behind the female fighter's blade and strikes her head with the long edge.

Alternatively, you can also Double from the outside with your short edge.

If your opponent parries the Doubling by going into the Crown…

… then take his foible and mutate to his lower opening.

The Displacements:
Confusion of Ideas

There are four basic guards, and each of these guards has a Displacement, or a certain technique for breaking this guard. The Displacements represent the best method for attacking each particular guard.

The Displacements are:

- The Crooked Strike breaks the Ox Guard
- The Cross Strike breaks the From the Roof Guard
- The Squinting Strike breaks the Plow Guard
- The Crown Strike breaks the Fool Guard

10.1 The Displacements

Liechtenauer's successors advised against parrying in combat, but they were referring to pure parrying and pushing away the opponent's blade, not the four Displacements. There are a number of techniques that can be used against fighters who like to use the parry. Liechtenauer and the later fencing masters summarized these under the umbrella term "the Devices against the Displacements." Unfortunately there is a slight confusion of ideas here, but in practice it is not so bad. Once again, an overview:

- The four Displacements break the four Guards.

- The Devices against the Displacements are the techniques that are used against fighters who parry.

- Deflecting is pure parrying or pushing away of the opposing blade.

The four Displacements are used to break the Guards. There are varying opinions as to how to understand the Displacements. In my opinion the Displacements are the best way to attack a fighter who changes in a particular Guard. If he is in the Guard, then I do not try to attack him with the Displacements, instead when the opportunity presents itself I force him to abandon the Guard and move. In the opinion of other swordsmen, the four Displacements are designed to permit effective attacks against fighters standing in one of the Guards. This is true only to a limited extent, however, in particular in the Displacement against the Fool – the Crown Strike – in practice it is almost impossible.

Another advantage of the four Displacements is that, not only do they break the four Guards, they are also well-suited to counter the obvious attacks from the various Guards. Therefore, if you are too late in making a Displacement against a Guard and your opponent attacks, then his attack should nevertheless be parried from your Master Strike.

In conclusion, there is another reason why the Displacements are so important: if one views the Guards not as postures or positions, but as designations for the place where the sword is, then the Displacements become even more important. So the fencing masters placed in our hands a means of determining with what we should strike while free fighting. For example, if during combat our opponent—for whatever reason—holds his sword by his right side, that is in a position roughly similar to the right Plow, we therefore know that we should attack with a Squinting Strike. During combat, therefore, we always have guidance as to how to attack the opponent. For this reason, very many areas of action open themselves for the Displacements, and one also understands why they were so important to the fencing masters.

THE FOUR DISPLACEMENTS

The Crooked Strike breaks the Ox Guard.

The Cross Strike breaks the From the Roof Guard.

The Squinting Strike breaks the Plow Guard.

The Crown Strike breaks the Fool Guard.

10.2 The Devices against the Displacements

THE TEAR (*Das Reissen*)

If the opponent deflects an over-cut, you move your hilt to the opponent's hands and tear his hands downwards. At the same time, you strike at the opponent's head. This is a very fast and effective technique. It is, however, only possible at close quarters.

THE SNAP (*Das Schnappen*)

You make a right under-cut, and your opponent falls on your sword. Now you snap over his sword and strike at his head. "Snapping" is a movement in which you make a forward and backward movement with the pommel, thus freeing your blade from the bind, and immediately strike. If your left under-cut is parried, strike at the opponent's head with your short edge.

The Snap can always be used when your blade is pushed downwards and back.

THRUST WITH THE HALF-SWORD (*Stich mit dem Halbschwert*)

You make a Strike of Wrath and your opponent parries. Simply strike a Cross Strike to the other side. During the Cross Strike, grasp your blade with your left hand in the center of the blade (Half-Sword) and thrust into his face or another of the four openings, depending on which works best. Take care to constantly maintain the maximum possible pressure. Should your opponent deflect this thrust, then attack him on the other side with a pommel blow, place your grip on the neck and throw him backwards.

THE TEAR

A device against the Displacement: the Tear. Your Strike of Wrath is parried in the near measure.

Hook your pommel over the opponent's right arm.

THE SNAP

Your under-cut is parried downwards strongly by your opponent.

Step 1	
ARMS:	You are in a close bind. Move your pommel over the opponent's right arm and push it downwards, while you strike his head with your long edge.
BODY:	Keep your upper body upright.
LEGS:	Step to the left beside the opponent's sword.

Step 1	
ARMS:	Your blade was pushed downwards, the point facing to the rear. Now snap forward under the opponent's blade and strike with energy at his head.
BODY:	Keep your upper body upright.
LEGS:	You can take a step, depending on the measure.

Now use your pommel to push his arms downward, while you strike his head.

Disengage the bind by briefly moving forward with your pommel.

As soon as the blades separate, immediately snap your blade at the opponent's head.

THRUST WITH THE HALF-SWORD

Your opponent parries your Strike of Wrath.

Break contact and with your hand grasp your blade at the mid-point.

Thrust from the other side into the opponent's face.

If the opponent parries your thrust …

… then strike with your pommel from the other side.

Alternately or in addition to the pommel blow, you can place your grip on the opponent's neck …

… and throw him backwards.

Step 1

ARMS: You are in the bind. Now move to the opposite side and deliver a Cross Strike. While you are moving to the opposite side, grasp your blade at the mid-point. Be sure that while in the bind, your opponent's direction of pressure is rather to the side and his point is aimed upwards. Create considerable pressure.

BODY: In this technique you must go around the opponent's blade. Depending on his blade position, you may have to bend your upper body backwards slightly to avoid it.

LEGS: From the bind, take a step to the left with your left leg.

Step 2

ARMS: Close his line of attack by bringing your blade between the opponent's blade and yourself, while thrusting at his head.

Step 3

ARMS: If your opponent parries the thrust, then strike at his head with the pommel from the other side.

Step 4

ARMS: Remain in the Bind and push his blade back somewhat, while striking at his head with your pommel.

BODY: Here once again you need to keep your upper body upright, so as to be able to generate sufficient force.

LEGS: Step around your opponent's blade again on your right side.

Step 5

ARMS: As an alternative to the blow or after the blow, place your grip against the opponent's neck and throw him backwards.

BODY: Turn your upper body, using the rotation to initiate the throw.

LEGS: If necessary, step your right foot back slightly, in order to be able to carry out a pulling movement.

Fighting at the Sword:
All's Fair

Often in combat you end up in a close or even a tight measure. That is the right time to begin "wrestling at the sword." In wrestling there are three basic areas: wrestling at the sword, combat wrestling and *Schlossringen*. The latter was a sporting variant and does not concern us here. Combat wrestling contains the complete arsenal of serious wrestling, with all the throws, levers, breaks and so on.

Wrestling is sometimes used in sword fighting when both opponents let their swords fall and continue fighting unarmed. Wrestling at the Sword is the intermediate stage to this. From normal combat, one begins wrestling, and one must not only concern oneself with throws, levers and breaks, but also with controlling the opponent's blade and whether or not to begin wrestling at all. Optimally, of course, the combat is decided in wrestling at the sword. All of the techniques illustrated here fall under the heading of wrestling at the sword, however only a few possibilities are shown here, to make the subject matter understandable.

Wrestling at the Sword usually begins with a running in or running through movement. Through these two techniques you will surely end up in a close measure, in order to begin Wrestling at the Sword. To be able to successfully wrestle at the sword, you must be close enough to the opponent to be able to get a good hold on him or throw him. As a rule, that is only the case in one situation: in the bind. If you are that close to the opponent without the weapons in contact, then you

do not have his sword under control, which means you are taking an increased risk. But you cannot begin wrestling from every bind. You should have bound forte against forte, either between you in a normal bind or over you in the Crown.

For the following explanations, we begin in the following situation: your approach results in you being in bind with your opponent. You are hard in bind, forte to forte. What happens next?

11.1 Downward Arm Lever

Wrestling at the Sword can also take place from a greater measure, if one prepares for it early enough. In this, as in all other leverage movements, it is very important to work fluidly and quickly.

This is how the pommel is hooked over the opponent's right arm. Be sure to continue maintaining cover with your blade.

DOWNWARD ARM LEVER

The fighters are standing in a close measure, forte to forte.

The fighter on the left reaches over the opponent's right hand with his pommel, while grasping the opponent's right elbow with his left hand.

The opponent is now forced to the ground with the arm lever.

Step 1	
ARMS:	Let go of the grip with your left hand and hook your grip over the right arm of your opponent. Simultaneously place your left hand on the opponent's right elbow.
LEGS:	Step your left leg forward, so that you are standing beside your opponent's arms.

Step 2	
ARMS:	Now pull his right hand to your right hip and back with your pommel, while with your left you push down directly on the elbow. You can now break the opponent's elbow.
BODY:	It is important to stay upright, for only in this way can you exert good downwards force.
LEGS:	During the lever, step back slightly with your right leg. The resulting rotation will increase the pressure.

11.2 Forward Arm Lever

If your opponent strikes hard with a right over-cut, you can step diagonally forward to the left. At the same time you close the opponent's line of attack, hook over his wrist and attack his elbow. You are thus in the starting position for the lever.

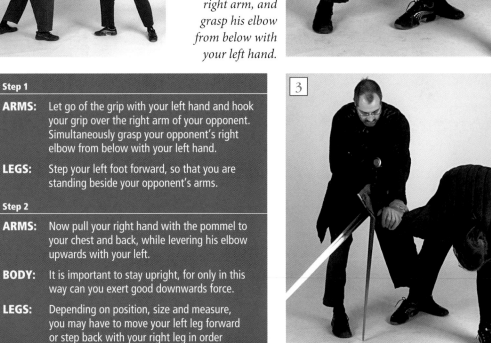

FORWARD ARM LEVER

The fighters are in a bind, forte on forte.

Hook your pommel over the opponent's right arm, and grasp his elbow from below with your left hand.

Step 1	
ARMS:	Let go of the grip with your left hand and hook your grip over the right arm of your opponent. Simultaneously grasp your opponent's right elbow from below with your left hand.
LEGS:	Step your left foot forward, so that you are standing beside your opponent's arms.

Step 2	
ARMS:	Now pull your right hand with the pommel to your chest and back, while levering his elbow upwards with your left.
BODY:	It is important to stay upright, for only in this way can you exert good downwards force.
LEGS:	Depending on position, size and measure, you may have to move your left leg forward or step back with your right leg in order to best execute the lever.

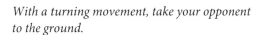

With a turning movement, take your opponent to the ground.

11.3 Reverse Grip Lever

This lever can also be executed well from the Crown, but only if your opponent is the same size or shorter than you. Against a larger opponent this techniques is not suitable from the Crown.

REVERSE GRIP LEVER

From the Bind, with your upside-down right hand reach under the opponent's right arm for his left arm.

While you take a step back with your left foot, pivot and throw him backwards. Of course in this situation you can also strike with the pommel.

Step 1	
ARMS:	Let go of the grip with your left hand and with your upside-down left hand grab the grip of the opponent's sword between his hands. If he is holding his hands together, then grab over the fingers of his left hand.
LEGS:	Step forward with your left foot, so that you are standing beside your opponent's arms.

Step 2	
ARMS:	Now wrench the opponent's sword down and to the left. In the process his sword turns so that, at the end, its point is pointing at the ground. You can throw him or strike at his head with the pommel.
BODY:	If is important to remain upright, for only thus can you execute the movement forcefully.
LEGS:	While you are turning his sword outwards, step back with your left leg. This rotation will give you the necessary force.

11.4 Throw to the Rear

The throw to the rear over the hip is very effective. Should you be lighter than your opponent, then for safety grasp the opponent's neck with the bend of your elbow. You must turn your left hand with the back of the hand facing down. In serious combat a short blow with the elbow to the opponent's throat would make him more submissive. During training, however, be concerned about your partner's safety.

THROW TO THE REAR

From the bind you step forward with your left leg, push the opponent's blade away and place your arm across his neck.

Throw your opponent backwards over your hip. Upright posture is important.

Step 1:	
ARMS:	Let go of the grip with your left hand, and control the opponent's blade with your own. Place your left arm across the opponent's neck.
BODY:	Bring your hip to the opponent's body.
LEGS:	Step forward with your left leg, so that it is behind the right leg of your opponent.

Step 2:	
ARMS:	Now throw the opponent backward. Be sure that you continue to control his blade.
BODY:	It is important to remain upright, for this is the only way to execute the movement powerfully. Turn your hips as you execute the throw.
LEGS:	There strength here comes from the rotation of your body, from the hips. Remain standing, for your opponent falls over your left leg.

11.5 Forward Arm Lever

In principle, this arm lever does not differ much from the downward arm lever. What is important here is the turning movement, which forces even stubborn opponents to the ground.

FORWARD ARM LEVER

From the Bind let your sword drop and grab the opponent's right wrist and right elbow from below.

Now lever your left elbow upwards and bring him to the ground.

Step 1:	
ARMS:	Let your sword drop, and grasp the opponent's right wrist with your right hand while seizing his right elbow from below with your left.
LEGS:	Move your left leg forward, so that you are standing beside the opponent's arms.

Step 2	
ARMS:	Now turn his elbow forward and pull his wrist back. Throw him forward to the ground.
BODY:	Remain as upright as possible. It is better to go to your knees than bend forward.
LEGS:	If your opponent does not go to the ground immediately, then kneel down. Move forward as you do so, so that your opponent falls on his face.

11.6 Throw to the Front

This throw works less well against opponents who are taller and/or heavier. Be sure to keep your center of gravity lower than your opponent's center of gravity. This throw can be difficult to execute without the use of your hip. Be especially sure to bring your hip as close to the opponent as possible.

Step 1	
ARMS:	Release the grip with your left hand and grasp your opponent around the ribcage from behind. Be sure to control his blade throughout the entire movement.
BODY:	Bring your hip as close to the body of your opponent as possible.
LEGS:	Step your left leg forward, so that you are standing in front of the opponent's legs.
Step 2	
ARMS:	Now throw your opponent forward with a turning motion.
BODY:	It is important to remain upright, for only thus can you execute the movement with power. Take the opponent on your hip.

FORWARD THROW

From the bind, step your left leg in front of the opponent's legs and grasp him around the ribcage from behind.

Take the opponent on your hip, and with a turning motion …

… throw him in front of you.

11.7 Throw with the Grip

The following techniques begin from the Crown. If both fighters come hard in bind, then it often happens that both end up in the Crown. The Crown is a reaction to the bind or to an attack in which the hilt is raised to protect the head. The Crown can be assumed with the point facing upwards or to the side. If two fighters in bind push hard against each other, then both often end up in a Crown.

THROW WITH THE GRIP

From the Bind, reach over the opponent's right arm for the grip of his sword with your inverted left hand.

Turn his sword outwards, while you step to the right and strike him in the head with your pommel.

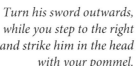

After the pommel blow place your grip over his neck and throw him to the ground.

Step 1	
ARMS:	Release the grip with your left hand, and with your left hand inverted reach over the opponent's right arm for the grip of his sword between his hands. If he has his hands together, then reach over the fingers of his left hand.
LEGS:	Step forward with your left leg, so that you are standing beside your opponent's arms.

Step 2	
ARMS:	Now wrench his sword out and upwards to the left. In doing so, turn his sword so that, in the end, its point is facing downwards. Strike his head with the pommel from the other side. Control his blade throughout.
BODY:	It is important to remain upright, for only thus can you execute the movement with power.
LEGS:	While you turn his sword outwards, step with your right leg to his left side. The resulting rotation will provide the necessary force.

Step 3	
ARMS:	After the pommel blow, place your grip on the front of his neck and throw him to the ground.

11.8 Arm Lever to the Rear

This outstanding leverage technique from the Crown is not only very fast, it is also extremely effective. Remember that this move can also be very painful.

Teach yourself this technique slowly to avoid injuries. This leverage technique can be used by both fighters.

REVERSE ARM LEVER

If both fighters are in a strong bind, it often happens that they both rise up at the same time and end up in the Crown position. The following techniques have the Crown as starting position.

Step 1	
ARMS:	Release the grip with your left hand. With the bend of your right elbow, block the opponent's right wrist. Now reach over the opponent's right arm with your left hand and grasp your own right forearm.
LEGS:	Step your left foot forward, positioning yourself close enough for this grasping movement.

Step 2	
ARMS:	Using the resulting leverage, push the opponent back and down. The Arm Lever is very painful if it is executed properly.
BODY:	If necessary, lean your body forward slightly.

Reach over the opponent's right arm with your left hand and then grab the bend of your right elbow. With your right forearm block the opponent's wrist.

Use the resulting leverage to force him backwards and down, and thus cause him to fall.

Here you see in detail how you reach over the opponent's arm to grasp the bend of your elbow.

When executing the Lever, be sure that your right leg blocks the opponent's legs.

11.9 The Scissors (*Die Schere*)

The Scissors is very painful if it is carried out correctly. Please be sure to practice this technique slowly and carefully. In the Scissors it is important to fix the opponent's forearm between your grip and your own forearm, by forcefully pushing your elbow out and forward.

THE SCISSORS

In the Crown position, place your grip laterally behind the opponent's right wrist. Grab his pommel, and be sure to close the scissors by moving the elbows outward.

With pressure on the bones in his forearm and a rotary motion, bring your opponent to the ground.

Step 1	
ARMS:	Let go of the grip with your left hand. Now place your grip on your opponent's right forearm. Grab the pommel on the other side with your left hand, as illustrated.

Step 2	
ARMS:	Now close the Scissors, by pulling your grip towards you and pushing your elbows slightly outward. This will cause pressure to build on your opponent's forearm.

Step 3	
ARMS:	With your grip, wrench your opponent's forearm downward. As you do so, rotate slightly to the left and exert strong pressure on his forearm.
LEGS:	If necessary, take a step back with your left leg.

In the Scissors your thumbs point outward. Be sure that you place your grip on the opponent's forearm and not his wrist.

11.10 Throw with the Blade

You are in a bind. With the short edge, wind at the opponent's face, causing him to parry. Then pull away to the other side, go into Half-Sword and from the left place your blade in front of his neck, then throw him backwards. Of course, this move will also work from a Crown.

One can also kick and punch from a bind in the Crown position. Kicks to the body, the knees or the genitalia are easy to carry out. Knee strikes are also very effective in a closer measure. Of course, at any time you can let go of the grip with one hand in order to strike. It is also very effective if you raise your pommel between the opponent's hands and strike him in the face. A pommel blow is also possible from a lower bind forte to forte. In this case you bypass the opponent's blade and strike him in the head.

THROW WITH THE BLADE / CLOSE COMBAT FROM THE BIND

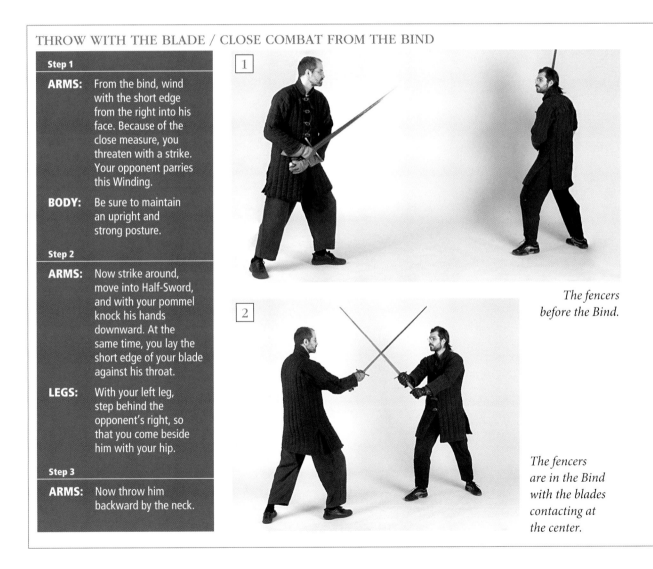

Step 1	
ARMS:	From the bind, wind with the short edge from the right into his face. Because of the close measure, you threaten with a strike. Your opponent parries this Winding.
BODY:	Be sure to maintain an upright and strong posture.
Step 2	
ARMS:	Now strike around, move into Half-Sword, and with your pommel knock his hands downward. At the same time, you lay the short edge of your blade against his throat.
LEGS:	With your left leg, step behind the opponent's right, so that you come beside him with your hip.
Step 3	
ARMS:	Now throw him backward by the neck.

The fencers before the Bind.

The fencers are in the Bind with the blades contacting at the center.

The fighters are in the Crown. From the Crown you can not only wrestle, but also kick and punch.

From the Bind, the fighter winds left with the short edge to the opponent's face. He parries.

… places the short edge of his blade on the opponent's throat …

Now the fighter on the left knocks the opponent's hands downward with his pommel, takes the Half-Sword …

… and throws him backward.

Pommel strike beneath the opponent's arms.

A direct pommel blow is also possible from a normal Bind.

Knee to the solar plexus.

Kick to the body.

Punch to the face.

"The Dürer," a kick to the genitals.

Kick to the knee.

Disarming Techniques:
Taking the Sword

As in every fighting art, there are also disarming techniques in long sword combat. Disarming is naturally closely related to wrestling at the sword. If the opponent does not let go of is weapon completely, strictly speaking it is no longer a successful disarming technique, but usually you will break his right wrist, an elbow, or force him to the ground. But in any case he loses control of his weapon. The disarming technique has thus become a wrestling technique, a lever. The transitions are therefore often fluid.

12.1 Sigmund Ringeck's Disarming Technique (1440)

If you and your opponent are in the bind, with your inverted left hand you grasp both blades where they touch. Meanwhile move your pommel over the opponent's right hand and wrench the swords toward you, up and to the right.

SIGMUND RINGECK'S DISARMING TECHNIQUE

1

The fighters have struck into a bind.

Grab the blades at the crossing point, so that the back of your hand is facing out and to the right.

2

Place your pommel over the opponent's right arm.

Now wrench both swords into a right Ox position, while you hold the swords at Half-Sword.

Step 1

ARMS: Your swords are together roughly at the mid-point. Now slide your inverted left hand upward along your blade, and grab both blades at the crossing point. At the same time, hook your pommel over the opponent's right wrist.

BODY: Keep your upper body straight.

LEGS: During the grabbing movement step forward with your left leg, so as to be in a good position to hook in.

Step 2

ARMS: Grip both blades securely, and hook your grip over the opponent's wrist. Abruptly wrench both swords with the hilt up and to the right, into an Ox position. Now, in Half-Sword, you are in a good thrusting position. Your opponent is also usually off balance.

BODY: Do not forget an upright body position, as it enables good power delivery and the ability to thrust or react immediately.

LEGS: To lend more force to the disarming move, step back with your right foot. The turning motion of your hips is necessary to develop force.

12.2 Peter von Danzig's Disarming Technique (1452)

In the bind, you reach over the opponent's right hand with your left hand, seize the grip between his hands, and with a step backward twist the sword our of his hand. This technique is also very well suited for use after Running In or from the Crown.

Step 1	
ARMS:	You are in the Bind, forte against forte. With your left hand palm-up, reach between the opponent's hands from above and seize his grip.
LEGS:	Step forward with your left leg in order to gain a good, secure grip.
Step 2	
ARMS:	Now wrench his sword back and to the left, pulling the grip from the opponent's hands.
BODY:	You must generate as much force as possible from the turning motion, otherwise you may not be able to wrench the sword from the opponent's grasp.
LEGS:	As you wrench the sword from your opponent's hands, again take a step back with your left leg.
Step 3	
ARMS:	Now strike as directly as possible at his now exposed opening. This technique knocks your opponent off balance. Even if you are unable to take the sword from his hands, you have time and opportunities enough to end the combat.

PETER VON DANZIG'S DISARMING TECHNIQUE

The fighters are in a close Bind, forte on forte.

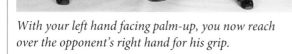

With your left hand facing palm-up, you now reach over the opponent's right hand for his grip.

With a turning motion and a small step back, you now wrench the sword from his hands.

12.3 Disarming Technique from the Codex Wallerstein (1470)

Your opponent attacks you with an over-cut. Let his sword slide by you (Hanging Point) and place your arm over his blade. In this way you pin the sword beneath your arm. You lever out his sword with your forearm, at the same time striking at his opening. This technique works best if you get hold of his cross guard.

DISARMING TECHNIQUE FROM THE CODEX WALLERSTEIN

The fighter on the right attacks with an over-cut. The fighter on the left allows the opponent's blade to slide off his own and reaches over its blade.

He jams the opponent's blade under his armpit.

More force is developed by seizing the cross guard.

Step 1		
ARMS:	Your opponent attacks with an over-cut. You run through and let his blade side down your own.	
LEGS:	Step straight toward the opponent with your left leg.	
Step 2		
ARMS:	As soon as the opponent's sword slides down yours, reach over his blade with your left arm and jam it firmly beneath your armpit. Continue the movement and place your forearm on the right side of the forte of the opponent's blade.	
Step 3		
ARMS:	Now lever the opponent's sword outward and simultaneously strike at his opening from the right.	
LEGS:	Step back with the left leg to generate the necessary force.	
Step 4		
ARMS:	The break in preparation for taking his sword.	
Step 5		
ARMS:	The opponent has clamped your sword under his arm in the manner described above.	
Step 6		
ARMS:	Now wrench your hilt downward and with your left hand simultaneously grasp your point.	
LEGS:	You must step forward to be able to lever effectively.	
Step 7		
ARMS:	Lever your opponent's arm backward.	

Then he pulls the opponent's blade outward while he strikes at the opening. Even if he cannot lever the blade from the opponent's hand, he will land a clean blow.

The break: the defender has clamped the sword under his arm.

Here you see the same lever from behind.

The attacker pulls his sword down and as a result has a lever.

The attacker moves the sword further and increases the pressure on the shoulder. The defender goes to the ground.

12.4 Paulus Hector Mair's Disarming Technique (1542)

The following technique sometimes results in disarming, but more often it ends with a lever that forces the opponent to the ground. The intent and purpose of disarming is loss of control over his weapon by the opponent. Even if he does not lose his weapon, he no longer has control of it.

Step 1	
ARMS:	In the bind, grasp both blades with your upturned hand. With your right hand, move your pommel over the opponent's wrist.
BODY:	Be sure to maintain a stable, upright stance.
Step 2	
ARMS:	Now hook your pommel down over the opponent's wrist.
BODY:	Remain as upright as possible, and turn your hips slightly to the rear. The rotation should be quick and powerful, forcing your opponent to the ground.
LEGS:	Support this rotation by simultaneously taking a step backward with the right leg.

PAULUS HECTOR MAIR'S DISARMING TECHNIQUE

The fighters are in the Bind, pressure is directed at them. Step forward to the left, while seizing the blades at the crossing point.

Hook your pommel over the opponent's right arm. Stepping back with your right leg …

… force your opponent to the ground. At the same time, slice at his neck from behind.

Fighting Powerfully: Stay in the Before

While a number of principles in the combat manuals are explained in detail, others are only comprehensible through comparisons and precise working out. In this chapter I would like to illustrate several of the most important principles.

13.1 The Four Hangings

The Hanging is a central aspect of the German school of sword fighting. In the Hangings the point is always aimed in the direction of the opponent, preferably at his face. A constant threat is maintained in this way.

Very many cuts and techniques end in a Hanging. For example, with the exception of the Crooked Strike, all of the Master Strikes end in Hangings. On the other hand, the Crooked Strike can easily be struck from all four Hangings. This once again offers many possibilities of tying up the Master Strikes.

In combat, always try to aim your point at the opponent. Not only does this give you the opportunity to thrust quickly at an opening, it also makes it difficult for the opponent to easily move to a close measure. You should always pose a threat to the opponent with which he must grapple. One way of achieving this is through consistent use of the four Hangings.

If you parry an opponent's under-cut, then allow your pommel to hang toward the ground so that the point is aimed at his face, and thrust into his face. If he parries an over-cut, then move upward with him and allow your point to hang down and thrust from above. One can use all three Wonders—Cut, Thrust and Slice—from the Hangings.

13.2 The Wheel (*Redel*)

The Wheel (*Redel* or *Rad*) is a technique that is used in the approach. In the Wheel, hold your sword in front of your with outstretched arms, your thumb on top on the flat of the blade. With your point, now describe an arc in front of you from left to right and back. Approach your enemy in this way. From this position you can immediately change through to either side if your opponent reacts to your Wheel. It also makes it difficult for your opponent to guess where you will now attack. When changing through, be sure to close the opponent's line of attack.

13.3 Pommel and Cross Guard

The sword consists of more than just the blade. You should never forget that when you are in combat. Wrenching techniques with the cross guard, blows with the pommel and also the popular Death Blow (*Mordschlag*) are not to be underestimated.

CROSS GUARD:
With your cross guard you can knock away, pull away or push away the opponent's blade. This usually only works in a tight measure, when your swords are forte on forte. In many techniques the opponent's blade is intercepted in a cross and is therefore held by your cross guard.

THE FOUR HANGINGS

Lower Hanging right.

Lower Hanging left.

Upper Hanging right.

Upper Hanging left.

Step 1	
ARMS:	The arms are kept relatively close to the body, in order to make an immediate thrust possible.
BODY:	Stand upright, only then can you react quickly and flexibly and, if necessary, lean into a thrust.
LEGS:	Your legs will be positioned differently, depending on from which movement you end up in a Hanging. It is important to have a good stance, from which quick reactions are possible.

THE FOUR HANGINGS

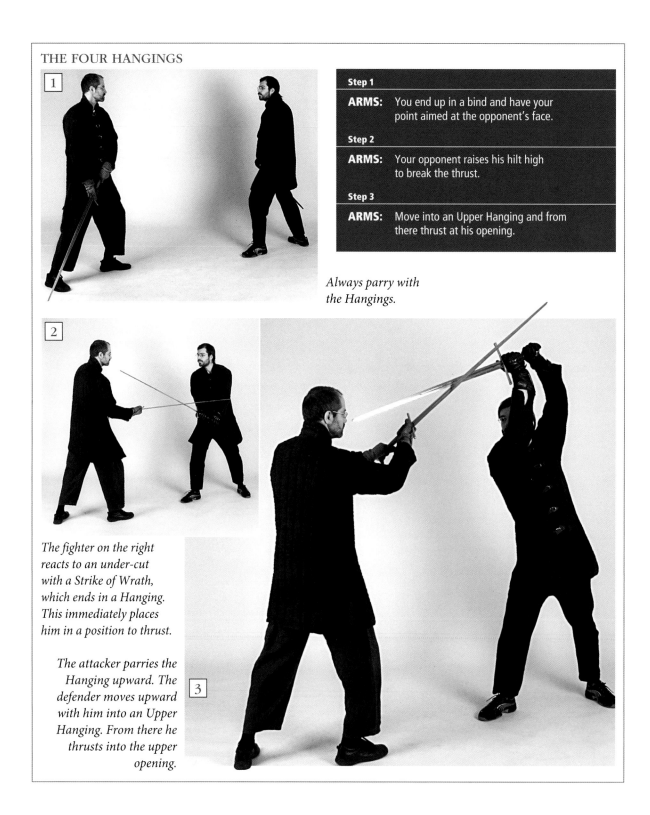

Step 1	
ARMS:	You end up in a bind and have your point aimed at the opponent's face.
Step 2	
ARMS:	Your opponent raises his hilt high to break the thrust.
Step 3	
ARMS:	Move into an Upper Hanging and from there thrust at his opening.

Always parry with the Hangings.

The fighter on the right reacts to an under-cut with a Strike of Wrath, which ends in a Hanging. This immediately places him in a position to thrust.

The attacker parries the Hanging upward. The defender moves upward with him into an Upper Hanging. From there he thrusts into the upper opening.

THE WHEEL

Hold your sword in front of you in Long Point, your thumb on top on the flat of the blade.

Step 1	
ARMS:	You are standing in a Long Point, your thumb is on top on the flat of the blade. Move the point back and forth in a circular motion as you approach the opponent. This forces him to do something. He will have to attack, with his attack directed against your blade.
BODY:	Be sure to have sufficient tension in your body to be able to thrust at any time.
LEGS:	Pay attention to your footwork. You should be able to rush forward at any moment in order to deliver a thrust.
Step 2	
ARMS:	As soon as your opponent makes an attack or attempts to bind your blade, change through and thrust at the opening on the other side.

Move the point back and forth in a circular motion.

If your opponent then attacks with an over-cut, allow him to strike, change through and thrust at his upper opening.

117

POMMEL (*Knauf*):

A pommel blow is usually very effective after you have knocked the opponent's blade out of the way with the cross guard. Blows with the pommel can be used in many situations. Here, too, of course, it is important to be in a close measure.

THE DEATH BLOW (*Mordschlag*):

A somewhat different technique is the so-called Death Blow, in which you use your sword as a club. You strike with the hilt. The weight of the hilt gives your blow tremendous power. Often your opponent is not expecting this attack, therefore you can strike through his cover. But caution: not only is the blow very powerful, it is also difficult to control. You can inflict serious injuries with it!

Should your opponent block the Death Blow, then push his blade downward with your cross guard and strike him in the face or solar plexus with your pommel.

Variants: Go into Half-Sword and swing your hilt at the opponent's head when he doesn't expect it. As the Half-Sword is a known fighting style, the opponent will assume that you will continue fighting in the Half-Sword. The blow with the pommel will therefore take him by surprise.

POMMEL BLOW

Pommel blow from the Crown by going under the arms of your opponent and then forward.

Knock the opponent's blade out of the way with the cross guard and follow with a pommel blow.

KNOCKING AWAY WITH THE CROSS GUARD

The fighters are in the Bind, the direction of pressure is slightly past the body.

Using his cross guard, the fighter on the right knocks the opponent's blade away to the right.

From the Knocking Away movement's end position, he quickly strikes the opponent's face with the pommel.

Step 1	
ARMS:	In the Bind, you knock the opponent's blade away to the side with your cross guard.
LEGS:	As you strike, take a step forward with your left leg. This brings you into a closer measure and lends added force to the blow.
Step 2	
ARMS:	In a flowing movement, from this blow with the cross guard you now thrust the pommel forward into the opponent's face.
BODY:	Lean slightly forward, in order to lend more force to the pommel blow.

THE DEATH BLOW

Grasp your sword by the blade and strike with the hilt.

Your opponent parries the Death Blow with a Double Block.

With your cross guard, push his sword downward …

… and thrust the pommel into his face.

Step 1	
ARMS:	Grasp the blade of your sword with both hands and then strike with the hilt.
Step 2	
ARMS:	Should your opponent block the attack, then push his sword away with the cross guard and strike with the pommel.
Step 3	
ARMS:	Alternately, you can strike with the hilt from the Half-Sword position by swinging it forward with one hand. You can also strike the knee from this position, for example.
INFO:	The name Death Blow is not without reason. Be very careful with it during training!

A VARIANT OF THE DEATH BLOW

1

The female fighter is in the Half-Sword position.

2

She threatens with a thrust.

3

The male fighter parries the thrust.

4

When the male fighter reacts, the female fighter lets go of her hilt and swings it at his head.

ATTENTION!
Be extremely cautious with this technique if you are in training. The blow is very powerful and if you land with your cross guard it can cause injuries even if your partner is wearing a fencing mask. Never underestimate the power of this blow.

13.4 Sweeping (*Streichen*)

Sweeping is based on the idea of deflecting the opponent's blade in order to then strike at an opening. Here you deflect the blade with a blow. Because you are practically striking from behind in the movement toward the opponent's blade, it is easy to get off track.

Fundamentally, you should Sweep better from the left side; from the right side the Sweep does not work as well. It is best to begin from a left Tail Guard. Now strike your opponent with a right over-cut, that is how you Sweep against his blade from the Tail Guard.

THE SWEEPING

Sweeping against an Over-Cut -- Step 1
(Illustrations 1 – 3)

ARMS: From the left Tail Guard, strike with your blade against the opponent's over-cut. Your short edge strikes the opponent's blade and knocks it away.

LEGS: Step back with your left leg.

Sweeping against an Over-Cut – Step 2

ARMS: Your opponent is in a weak bind, and his blade was knocked away.

Sweeping against an Over-Cut – Step 3

ARMS: Immediately strike at his blade from above with the long edge. As you do so, cover his line of attack by striking slightly to the right.

LEGS: If necessary, you can take a small step to the left if needed.

Your Opponent Binds Strongly – Step 1
(Illustrations 4 – 8)

ARMS: Your opponent is in a strong bind and pushes on your blade from above.

Your Opponent Binds Strongly – Step 2

ARMS: Double to his head. You can double with either the short or the long edge.

Your Opponent Winds against your Sweep – Step 1
(Illustrations 9 – 13)

ARMS: In the Bind your opponent moves upward and attempts to Wind.

Your Opponent Winds against your Sweep – Step 2

ARMS: Step back and strike at his right side with outstretched arms.

LEGS: Step straight back.

Your Opponent Falls on your Sword from Above – Step 1
(Illustration 14)

ARMS: Your opponent moves upward, in order to fall upon your sword from above.

Your Opponent Falls on your Sword from Above – Step 2

ARMS: Modify your Sweep slightly, and strike at his arms and hands from below.

You Sweep Through – Step 1
(Illustrations 16 – 22)

ARMS: You strike through with a Sweep on the other side.

You Sweep Through – Step 2

ARMS: Fall on his sword with your long edge, Wind into a left Ox, and strike the right side of his neck with your long edge and forte. Throw the opponent over your leg.

LEGS: Step behind is left leg with your right and throw him over it.

You can best Sweep from the left Tail Guard. Here the fighter on the left is attacking, while the one on the right is defending with Sweeps.

In the Sweep, you strike the opponent's blade from below with your short edge, thus deflecting his blade.

If his blade is knocked out of the way, then immediately strike at his opening from above with the long edge.

Your opponent binds your Sweep strongly.

Then simply Double behind his blade.

123

Your opponent binds your Sweep strongly.

Allow your point to hang slightly on your left side …

… and strike his head from the other side. Be sure to cover the line of attack and step to the right.

You Sweep against an attack …

… and your opponent goes up and attempts to Wind.

Pull back, while striking his hands from the right side.

Your opponent attempts to Wind.

If your opponent now attempts to pull away for a blow from the other side, then pull back while striking his left side on his arm.

If your opponent raises his arms to escape you Sweep, then strike his arms from below.

Your opponent keeps his arms low, in order to fall upon your blade.

Sweep through on the other side …

… and from there thrust at the opponent's chest. It is important here to cover the line of attack.

If the opponent holds his arms low, this gives you the opportunity to Sweep on the other side

You Sweep through on your right side.

In this case Wind into a left Ox ...

... and lay the short edge against his neck. While doing so you can take his blade with your cross guard.

If your long edge is against his neck, then throw him backward.

Practical Combat:
Techniques and Tactics

If we are facing an opponent in combat, then we must consider several aspects of techniques and fundamentals that have not yet been addressed. We are concerned here with the way in which a combat can be conducted. This chapter is obviously not complete and it never can be, as each fighter has his own views, experiences, and characteristics and has developed his own fighting style. Here, I would only like to point out several thoughts that I have personally recognized as important and helpful. Obviously many fighters will not agree with the theses presented here and will be of a different opinion, and that is a good thing. I therefore make no claim to completeness or correctness.

14.1 The Approach (*Zufechten*)

The combat begins in the Approach distance, when you and your opponent cannot yet reach each other. Several very important things play a role in this phase: your posture, your guards and your movements provide information about your style of fighting. You can appear threatening or also seem completely harmless. You can influence the impression your opponent has from the measure. Take the Approach seriously, for often it by itself will decide the outcome. You should consciously use and control the impression you create during the Approach. A strong approach impresses some fighters, while against others it is useful to appear non-threatening, indeed almost detached. Learn to assess your opponent.

14.2 The Withdrawal (*Abzug*)

By Withdrawal, we mean the safe stepping away from the opponent. After you have landed a blow, the combat is not over. Be sure to make a clean Withdrawal. Maintain constant cover as you move out of the measure. Just because you have struck an opponent does not mean that he cannot also land a blow or complete a movement he has begun. It is therefore also important to consider and to cover lines of attack.

14.3 Modifying the Strike of Wrath

It is not without reason that the Strike of Wrath is the most important Master Strike. It is the quickest, most powerful and versatile of the five cuts, and in particular it is a quick change artist. These qualities should be exploited in combat. Ringeck advises us right-handers to begin combat with a right Strike of Wrath, but he prudently says nothing about how we should follow up this Strike of Wrath. During execution, a Strike of Wrath can be modified into a Crosswise, Squinting or even Crooked Strike. Like the Strike of Wrath, the Squinting Strike is begun from a From the Roof Guard. Crosswise and Crooked Strikes from the Strike of Wrath are somewhat weak, but for that they are struck all the more quickly. By retaining the forward movement, one can easily break an opponent's parry with a Cross Strike. Under no circumstances, therefore, should we always resort rigidly to a Strike of Wrath. Instead we should always maintain control so that we are able to redirect the Strike of Wrath into another cut.

14.4 Half Step (*Halbschritt*)

When you have made the decision to attack, then start with a half step with the front leg. With this half step you adjust your measure from the opponent. At the same time you bring your blade into a menacing position, The Scales for example. The sole purpose of this half step is to cause your opponent to move. If your opponent moves, then you adjust your next movement with a complete step. This buys you the necessary time.

An example: you take a Half Step toward the opponent and at the same time move your blade forward, point first. As he assumes that you are attempting to thrust, your opponent will take a step to the side and try to parry your blade with a Crooked Strike. Now change through downward, for you have been waiting for the opponent's reaction.

14.5 Announce (*Anmelden*)

If you draw back your point, transfer your weight, turn your hips or shoulders, then you are announcing your attack. Your opponent will be able to react to it quickly. You should attempt to strike and thrust seamlessly. Be sure that your opponent cannot tell exactly when you are beginning an attack.

14.6 Measure (*Mensur*)

Each fighter has his own measure that suits him very well. You should attempt to fight in this measure and prevent the opponent from getting into his own measure. Handling the measure is very important, beginning with the Approach. If, for example, you are in a Long-Point, then keep the opponent at bay optically. If you are in a Plow Guard or even a Tail Guard, then reduce the measure optically. Often the feeling for the measure originates from the point of the blade. If you are in a Long-Point and leave the blade where it is, but go forward along the blade into a Plow, then your opponent still sees the blade in the same spot, even though you are in a much closer measure. If you do this without being noticed, then you have gained much distance without the knowledge of your opponent.

Simultaneous with the Half-Step, the fighter moves his blade forward in order to provoke a reaction to which he can respond. By reacting, the opponent reveals an opening that can be attacked.

The Half-Step with the front leg. The fighter is making this Half-Step from the Plow. At the same time he moves his blade forward and thus creates the impression of a threat.

Measure: A fighter in Long-Point keeps his opponent at a distance optically.

A small shifting of your legs can also bring a great deal of distance. Move your front leg just a few centimeters forward and that will greatly increase your range. This move can be efficiently camouflaged by a movement, for example while you are changing guards. Try this in training and play with the measure. You will appreciate very quickly the importance of handling the measure. During training, be sure to repeatedly attack from a long measure. A good fighter will usually attack from a distance of one and a half steps.

14.7 Strike Over the Bind

When you strike a Strike of Wrath in the Bind ("zeroing-in the point"), try to continue the Strike of Wrath so that, while maintaining a strong bind, you strike over the opponent's blade. In the Bind you must pull the pommel slightly to your right forearm and practically strike at the opponent over his sword. Even if your blade is tied up in combat, you should always check whether you cannot still "strike through."

Measure: A fighter in a Tail Guard takes away optical distance and can thus move closer to his opponent without appearing threatening.

Try to strike or thrust over the opponent's blade at his opening or force his blade away by Winding. Only if that does not work should you decide on another tactic. Of course that means that you intentionally strike hard in the Bind and maintain the Bind. When your opponent feels this pressure, he cannot simply yield if you are standing in the correct measure. You are therefore massively in the Before, and from there you either work over or on the opponent's blade.

14.8 The Important Lines

CENTER LINE (*Mittellinie*):
Every fighter has a center line. This should always be pointed at the opponent. It is the line in which you have the greatest power delivery. Always keep your center line pointed at the opponent!

LINE OF ATTACK (*Angriffslinie*):
The line of attack is a line of movement on which the attack moves. If you execute an attack or a counter-technique, be sure that your attack closes the opponent's line of attack to the extent possible. If, for example, after disengaging from the Bind upward strike downward, then do it in such a way that your opponent cannot strike at you from the left side. You close his line of attack by striking slightly to the right.

POINT LINE (*Ortlinie*):
If you have the point aimed at the opponent's face and then move it toward him with no bobbing movement, then you make it difficult for him to judge the strike or thrust. The strike or thrust will be perceived subjectively as very quick and will often be unpredictable. Essentially you push your blade in front of you in the direction of the opponent. From a Plow you push your blade forward without raising or lowering it. At the last moment you make a short, quick Twitch by pulling back the pommel. Ticks, in particular, can be executed very effectively with this technique.

The Center Line should always be aimed at the opponent. If you step out of this line, it means nothing more than you have aimed your Center Line at the opponent at a new angle.

THE "POINT LINE" OR "POINT HEIGHT"

Point Line

Move the sword straight forward without raising or lowering it.

Middle Line

131

In Direct Contact:
Possibilities from the Bind

The Bind is described over and over again in the combat manuals. If a fighter opens the fight with an attack, then either he strikes, the defender evades, or he concerns himself with the attack. The blades touch, the fighters are in a Bind. What can then be done from this binding of blades?

15.1 Analysis of the Situation

Most important is "Feeling." It is a matter of determining instantly where the direction or pressure lies, or in what direction the opponent's blade and your blade are pushing. Here, of course, there are four stages. We roughly differentiate between:

- The pressure goes straight toward you
  Techniques: Winding, Mutating, Running Through / Wrestling

- The pressure goes to the side
  Techniques: Changing Through, Twitching, Moving Away, Doubling, pulling away from a blow for another to the opposite side, Pommel Blow

- The pressure goes downward
  Techniques: Snapping, Changing Through

- There is no pressure
  Techniques: Thrusting, Winding, Mutating

An important question is: where are the points? The position of the points is decisive for subsequent possibilities. Here, too, one can roughly differentiate between:

- A point is aimed at a fighter
  Technique: Thrust

- No point is aimed at a fighter, the fighters are standing between the points
  Techniques: Winding, Mutating

- No point is aimed at a fighter, the points are beside the fighters
  Techniques: Changing Through, Twitching, Moving Away, Doubling, Striking Around, Running Through / Wrestling, Pommel Blow

Equally important is the question: where does the Bind take place? There are four different possibilities (always seen from the fighter's point of view):

- Forte on foible (= your forte is on the opponent's foible)
  Techniques: Moving Away, Winding, Thrusting

- Forte on forte
  Techniques: Snapping, Running Through, Pommel Blow, Doubling

- Foible on forte
  Techniques: Twitching, Changing Through, Striking Around

- Foible on foible
  Techniques: Winding, Changing Through, Moving Away

Finally, you should determine: is the opponent hard or soft in the bind? You can usually tell this from the direction of pressure, the position of the point and the amount of pressure.

The male fighter's point is aimed at the female fighter's face, her point is pointing to the side.

The points are to the right and left of the male fighter. The female fighter looks between the points.

The female fighter's point is aimed at the male fighter's face, his point is pointing to the side.

Both points are beside the fighters, the female fighter is very hard in the Bind.

Both points are beside the fighters, the male fighter is very hard in the Bind.

THE FOUR POSSIBLE BINDS

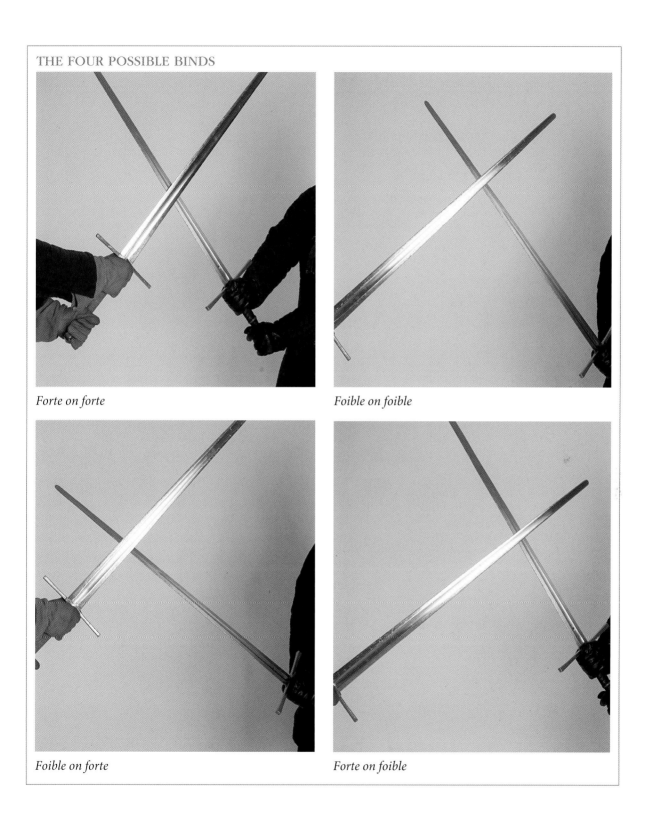

Forte on forte

Foible on foible

Foible on forte

Forte on foible

15.2 Practical Example:
A Technique from the Bind

You land in the Bind and your opponent obviously wants to strike hard over the Bind at your head, or zero-in the point. Parry his sword with your blade and push into the parry. This will tempt him to pull away for another blow to the opposite side. If he does, then place your blade with the edge on his left shoulder or neck. Be sure that you end up under his blade. Obviously at this point you strike a blow, but you can also follow it up with a slice.

CROSS STRIKE UNDER A MOVE TO STRIKE FROM THE OTHER SIDE

1

The fighters are facing each other.

2

The fighter on the left parries the attack forcefully to the left with his short edge.

3

Step 1	
ARMS:	In the Bind, push his blade outward forcefully with your edge. Your opponent will try to strike around.
BODY:	As soon as he lifts his blade to strike around, place the short edge of your sword on his neck. Be sure to hold your hilt high to cover his line of attack. If you do this correctly, then you are under the opponent's blade, and his blow will now press your blade into his neck.
LEGS:	Make sure to have an upright, stable posture.

The fighter on the right attempts to strike over the Bind at the head of the fighter on the left.

He parries this forcefully to the left with his short or long edge.

The fighter on the right now strikes around with a Cross Strike. The fighter on the left places his blade on the neck of the other fighter. The shorter path places him under the opponent's blade.

15.3 The Talking Window (*Das Sprechfenster*)

The Talking Window is the situation in which you and your opponent are in the Bind. You have come together with the long edges, and are standing in a strong bind with arms more or less extended. You should now feel what your opponent is doing or even planning. At the same time, you should grasp the entire situation and react to it. Of course, this is only possible, if at all, after years of intensive training. But that is no reason not to begin practicing today.

I therefore advise you to always to go into the Talking Window consciously and then try to feel what you should do in the situation you are in. If the enemy binds at the sword, stay in a strong Bind and see what the opponent does. If he attempts to thrust, follow him, if he tries to pull away upward, then make a cut against it, if he tries to execute a Cross Strike, then fall on his arms or strike a Cross Strike beneath his. If he does nothing, then try to attack his openings by Doubling or another maneuver.

THE FOUR POSSIBILITIES OF THE BIND

You and your opponent are standing in the Talking Window.

You are standing in the Talking Window and "feel" your opponent.	Your opponent tries to strike around from the Bind.
Step 1	**Step 3**
ARMS: Your opponent now tries to thrust from the Bind. Follow up with a thrust.	**ARMS:** As soon as your opponent breaks the Bind to strike around, make a Cross Strike beneath his.
Step 2	**Step 4**
ARMS: React immediately, if you feel that he is changing his Bind. Wind your blade against his, thus forcing away the thrust, and thrust into his opening.	**ARMS:** Your opponent can also try to pull away upward from the Bind.
	Step 5
	ARMS: As soon as your opponent raises his blade, either strike under his arms, if you are quick enough, or on his arms.
	LEGS: Also take a small step with your left leg.

If your opponent (on the right in the photo) attempts to thrust, then follow up with a thrust of your own.

If your opponent attempts to strike around with a Cross Strike, then come under his Cross Strike.

If your opponent attempts to pull away upward …

… then fall on his arms.

Master Cuts in Practice:
Complex Combat Sequences

16.1 The Strike of Wrath

The Strike of Wrath is the most important Master Strike of all. The Strike of Wrath is always struck in the Hang, that means the blow is not struck through rather it ends in a position similar to the Plow with the point aimed at the opponent. In this way you always pose a threat, even if the Strike of Wrath is struck too short or the opponent evades by stepping back. You should always try to aim the point at the opponent. The Strike of Wrath is also one of the most common possibilities for achieving Bind.

EXAMPLE: Both fighters are in a guard. In the photos both are in the From the Roof Guard. The attacker begins with a Strike of Wrath from the right. The defender strikes a Strike of Wrath against it and steps slightly out of line. Both fighters are now in Bind. Of course there are many ways one can respond to a Strike of Wrath. Here, however, the defender strikes a Strike of Wrath, in order to come into Bind and work further from there.

If you end up in Bind as a result of a Strike of Wrath, then you can use various techniques depending on the type of Bind. The possibilities are explained in Chapter 14.

MOVE AWAY UPWARD: If you end up in Bind as a result of a Strike of Wrath, then not only can you thrust, but also Move Away Upward. This involves pulling your sword up and away, disengaging the bind, and then immediately striking from above, down at the opponent's head. When Moving Away Upward, it is important to close the line of attack in order to cover yourself.

THE STRIKE OF WRATH

Strike of Wrath – Point:
The fighters are standing in their guards.

An attack with a Strike of Wrath is countered with a Strike of Wrath, and the fighters are standing in the Bind. The female fighter on the right is in a weak bind, which is why the attacker's point is in front of her face.

From the Bind, the attacker simply thrusts at the face by the shortest path.

You can also strike the opponent with a Strike of Wrath over the Bind.

Step 1

ARMS: Technique: Strike of Wrath – Point: The attacker's point is aimed at the defender's face, her point is facing outward. The female defender is thus in a weak Bind.

Step 2

ARMS: Pressure in the Bind is maintained, and with the blades together you now thrust straight ahead into the defender's face.

BODY: It may be necessary to lean your body slightly forward to lend more power to the thrust.

LEGS: Should your opponent be too far away, the make a half step forward with the front leg.

Step 3

ARMS: Breaking the Strike of Wrath – Point: parry to the side. If the female defender feels threatened by a thrust, or she sees the danger, then she parries the opponent's blade to the side.

MOVE AWAY UPWARD

The fighters are facing each other in their guards.

The attacker feels the pressure from the female fighter and pulls his blade upward along her blade, which causes her to drop her blade to her left side.

Again an attack with a Strike of Wrath is answered. The female fighter on the left is hard on the sword, and as a result both points are beside the fighters. She pushes her blade and the blade of the attacker out and to the left— from her point of view.

Now the attacker simply strikes downward at her head. Because of the strong Bind, the female fighter lowers her hands and blade.

Step 1	
ARMS:	You are standing in the Bind. Your opponent is medium to strong, his direction of pressure is down and to the side.
LEGS:	Depending on the measure, you can also take a step here. It is advisable to step slightly to the left, especially when closing the line.
Step 2	
ARMS:	Pull the blade upward, so that you break the Bind, and immediately strike downward on the other side. Your opponent will either drop his sword outward or downward, or you will have to close his line of attack.

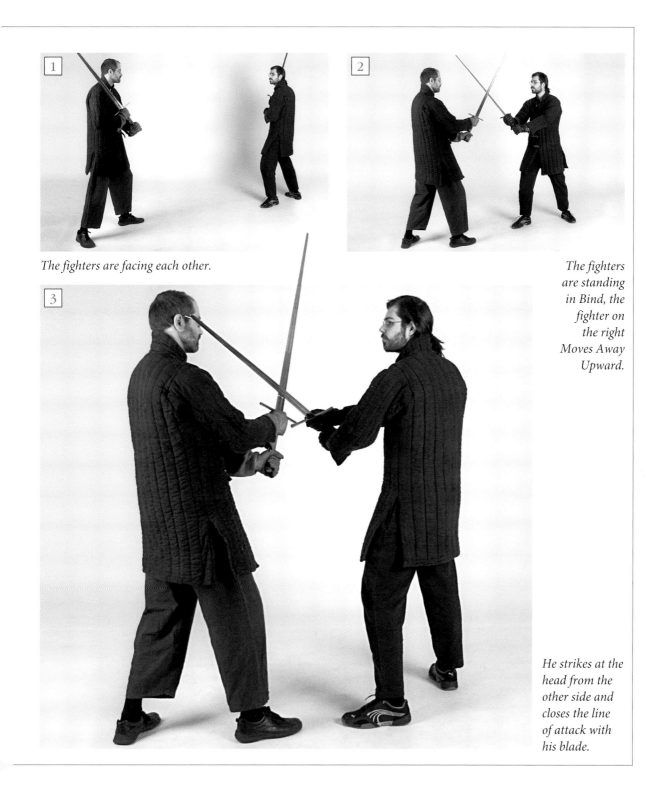

1

The fighters are facing each other.

2

The fighters are standing in Bind, the fighter on the right Moves Away Upward.

3

He strikes at the head from the other side and closes the line of attack with his blade.

16.2 The Crown Strike

The Crown Strike is a Master Strike that offers the least possibilities in action. It is mainly used to Run Over. Sometimes you can also use it to strike over cover.

The attacker makes a Crown Strike and the defender parries it upward. The attacker now raises his hilt and thrusts at the defender's chest. Of course this only works if the relative sizes and the Crown permit it (see Illustration 3).

BREAK: The Crown generally breaks the Crown Strike, but other over-cuts as well. If the defender parries the attack upward with the hilt, then he is standing in the Crown. The attacker can now go under the defender's hands and make a cut. The attacker should now push the hands upward and keep them under control. Then, in a flowing movement, he can step to the right and push the hands away in such a way that his sword comes down on the opponent's hands.

The fighter on the left attacks with a Crown Strike.

The female fighter parries this …

Step 1	
ARMS:	You strike a Crown Strike, which your opponent parries with the Crown.

Step 2	
ARMS:	Come under the opponent's arms with the long edge. Push the arms up and back.
LEGS:	Take a step toward the opponent in order to stand really close to his arms. Only in this way can you exert enough force. This should happen quickly, however.

Step 3	
ARMS:	Push the opponent's arms down and to the side while stepping to the side. Slice during the entire movement.
LEGS:	You move to the side where your point is. Depending on the measure, take a full or a half step.

Step 4	
ARMS:	Continue slicing, and push the opponent's arms further downward. In the end you are standing as in Illustration 7. From this position you can now also make a thrust if you want to.
LEGS:	At the end step back slightly, so that you are standing in a safe measure.

... and the male fighter thrusts over her parry to her opening.

The male fighter comes under her arms and pushes them upward.

While maintaining pressure, he moves to the side and slices along her arms.

The female fighter parries the Crown Strike with the Crown.

In the end his blade is lying on her arms and he is at a safe measure.

16.3 The Squinting Strike

The Squinting Strike is a very versatile and important Master Strike. It is used often, for it offers the opportunity to fight in the Meanwhile. Because it forces the opposing blade away, offers a high level of safety, for even in the worst case – should the Squinting Strike not work – one ends up in a Bind.

The attacker begins the combat with a Strike of Wrath. The defender strikes a Squinting Strike against it, so that the short edge strikes the attacker's shoulder. Very good balance and a good stance are important here. It results in the attacker's sword being forced out of line. The defender is standing in safety behind his blade. Should the Squinting Strike not land, one can immediately thrust from the end position.

SQUINTING STRIKE AGAINST LONG POINT:
If the opponent is standing in Long Point in front of you, then look him in the face while executing a Squinting Strike on his blade. He may be surprised by your blow. You're your short edge, strike hard against his foible, and immediately and without hesitation thrust at his chest.

SQUINTING STRIKE AGAINST THE THRUST:
In principle, the Squinting Strike functions against the thrust in the same way as the Squinting Strike against the Long Point.

SQUINTING STRIKE ON THE HANDS:
The attacker makes an over-cut. The defender looks at the attacker's head as if he intends to strike him there, but instead strikes a Squinting Strike against the attacker's blow and hits him in the hands with the point of the sword.

SQUINTING STRIKE AGAINST AN OVER-CUT

The male fighter attacks with a Strike of Wrath. The female fighter responds with a Squinting Strike and strikes him on the shoulder.

If she has selected too great a measure, while she fails to strike him, she is in a good thrusting position.

Step 1

ARMS: Strike a Squinting Strike at the opponent's foible. If your Squinting Strike misses the opponent because you are standing too far away, then maintain blade contact and slide forward along the opponent's blade. Then thrust at his upper opening.

BODY: Keep your upper body upright.

LEGS: Pay attention to your footwork, as, depending on the measure, you may have to cover a greater distance.

SQUINTING STRIKE AGAINST LONG POINT

The male fighter is standing in the Long Point position.

The Break: The female fighter strikes the Long Point with a Squinting Strike.

Step 1

ARMS: Your opponent is in front of you in the Long Point position. Look in his face, and strike this Long Point with a Squinting Strike. .

Step 2

ARMS: Stay in the binding and slide the blade of your opponent forward as you thrust. Do this quickly and in a smooth, continuous action.

LEGS: Make a necessary half-step forward to give a powerful thrust.

When using the Squinting Strike against the Long Point, it is easy to step slightly to the right. A double-hit is excluded.

She stays on the blade to be able to feel the opponent's actions and immediately after the Squinting Strike thrusts at his opening.

ORIGINS OF THE TERM "SQUINTING STRIKE"

Look (squint) at your opponent's head …

… but strike at his hands.

Step 1	
ARMS:	Your opponent strikes at you with an over-cut. Look into his face and strike his hands with a Squinting Strike.
LEGS:	You must step somewhat more to the side forward in order to evade his blow.

16.4 The Crooked Strike

The attacker begins the combat with a right over-cut or under-cut. The defender leaps to his right, out of the attack's path. At the same time, he strikes a Crooked Strike to the left at the opponent's hands or blade. The cut is made with the long edge, with the point to the left. If the blow strikes the opponent's blade, from there the defender immediately strikes the opponent's head with the short edge.

Alternately, after the Crooked Strike one can Wind to the opponent's sword with the short edge and thrust at the upper opening. Here the Crooked Strike can most easily be struck from a Barrier or Tail Guard.

BREAK 1: If the defender strikes a Crooked Strike on the attacker's blade, the attacker remains hard on the sword and, with a movement similar to a Doubling, thrusts under the opponent's blade at his opening. This only works if the Crooked Strike intercepts the over-cut in a high position.

BREAK 2: If the defender knocks the attacker's blade almost to the ground with a Crooked Strike, the attacker goes into a right or left Ox and thrusts at the defender's upper opening. Should the defender parry this, then the attacker remains in his Ox position and thrusts from one opening to the other, until he has ended the exercise or withdraws.

Crooked Strike against Long Point: If the opponent is standing in front of you in the Long Point position, then strike a Crooked Strike in the middle of his blade. From there, immediately strike at his head with the short edge of the sword. Be sure to cover the opponent's line of attack.

THE CROOKED STRIKE

The fighter on the left attacks with an over-cut.

The female fighter strikes his hands with a Crooked Strike.

Alternately, she can also twist his blade …

… and from there strike at his head with the short edge.

If she wants to be certain that the opponent cannot strike upward, then she should cover his line of attack.

THE CROOKED STRIKE

Step 1

ARMS: Strike a Crooked Strike against your opponent's over-cut.

LEGS: Be sure to step out of the way to the right.

Step 2

ARMS: Immediately after the Crooked Strike, strike at the head with the short edge.

Step 3

ARMS: Break: The attacker remains in a strong Bind against the Crooked Strike. That takes some getting used to, as one must move upward into a Bind immediately after an over-cut.

Step 4

ARMS: From this Bind, thrust under the defender's blade at his opening with a technique similar to a Doubling. You tilt your point toward the opening and push the pommel outward under your right elbow. Be sure to cover the line.

LEGS: Here you take a step forward.

Step 5

ARMS: Break: If the defender strikes your over-cut almost to the ground with a strong Crooked Strike, then go into the Ox position and thrust from there. Should this thrust be parried, then simply continue attacking with thrusts at the various openings.

BODY: Be absolutely sure to maintain good body position, otherwise you will be unable to strike powerfully from one opening to the other without losing your balance.

The fighters are standing in their guards.

The fighter on the right strikes a Crooked Strike on the blade. The defender on the left remains in a string bind from below ...

... and thrusts under the opponent's blade at his opening. As he does so he steps forward with his left leg.

The defender on the right has knocked the attacker's blade downward with a Crooked Strike.

The attacker goes into a right Ox and thrusts at the opening.

If the defender parries this thrust …

7

... then the attacker
simply changes
the opening he
is attacking.

8

He alternately attacks the left and right openings ...

9

... as well the upper and lower.

CROOKED STRIKE AGAINST LONG POINT: COMMON MISTAKES

The fighter on the left is standing in the Long Point position.

The fighter on the right strikes a Crooked Strike on the foible of the opponent's blade. The impact point is too far forward in the foible, and the defender does not step out far enough to the right. He is thus in extreme danger if he breaks the Bind. The fighter on the left only needs to take a step and aim his point, then the thrust is perfect.

In order to properly execute this break against the Long Point, the fighter on the right should twist in the middle of the blade and step out to the right. Only then can he close the line of attack if he subsequently strikes at the head.

16.5 The Cross Strike

The attacker makes a right over-cut. The defender jumps to his right, and while moving he brings his hilt over his head and strikes the opponent's head with the short edge. It is important to keep the arms extended in front of the body and, to the extent possible, keep the hilt over the head. In the process, the attacker's over-cut may be blocked by the cross guard. The attacker's blade is taken by the forte of the defender's blade. Of course this also works on the left side, although here the strike is made with the long edge.

BREAK:
Should the attacker parry your Cross Strike, then the defender Doubles behind his blade and strikes the opponent on the head or slices through his face.

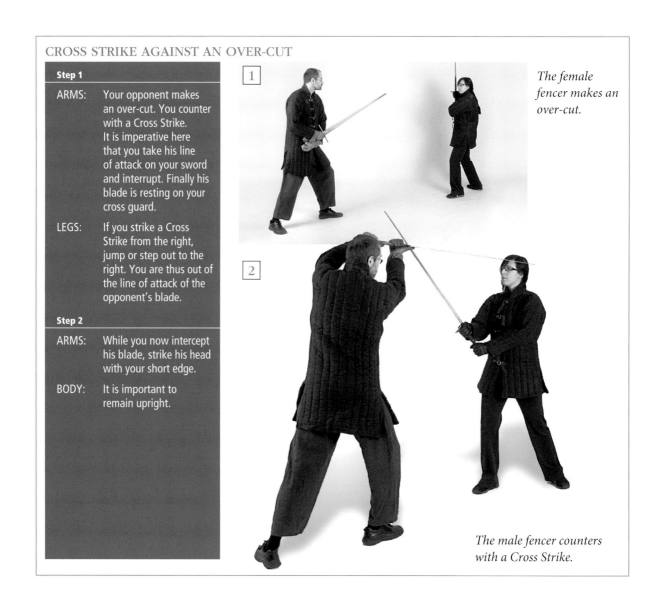

CROSS STRIKE AGAINST AN OVER-CUT

Step 1

ARMS: Your opponent makes an over-cut. You counter with a Cross Strike. It is imperative here that you take his line of attack on your sword and interrupt. Finally his blade is resting on your cross guard.

LEGS: If you strike a Cross Strike from the right, jump or step out to the right. You are thus out of the line of attack of the opponent's blade.

Step 2

ARMS: While you now intercept his blade, strike his head with your short edge.

BODY: It is important to remain upright.

The female fencer makes an over-cut.

The male fencer counters with a Cross Strike.

VARIANTS:

If the attacker is in a weak Bind, then strike directly at his head. If, however, he is in a weak Bind and outside your range, then as defender lay your short edge on the attacker's neck, step your left leg behind the attacker's left leg and throw him over it.

A BREAK AGAINST THE STRIKE AROUND:

The attacker attacks with a Cross Strike, the defender parries it. The first Cross Strike can also be a defense against an over-cut. The attacker now strikes around with a Cross Strike to the other side. The defender likewise makes a Cross Strike. In this way he beats the attacker to the punch and comes under his blade. It is important that the defender strikes a right Cross Strike if the attacker makes a left Cross Strike. The defender must keep his arms high to block the opponent's blade.

CROSS STRIKE AGAINST AN OVER-CUT

1

If the female fighter parries the Cross Strike …

… then the fighter Doubles her behind her blade. As he does so, he lowers his hilt slightly.

2

Step 1

ARMS: If your opponent parries the Cross Strike, Double behind his blade to his head, while keeping your arms somewhat low.

LEGS: Depending on the measure, you can take a step with the left leg.

A THROW FROM THE CROSS STRIKE

Step 1	
ARMS:	If your Cross Strike misses the opponent, but he is in a weak Bind, then place your short edge against the right side of his neck. You must turn the sword slightly to do so.
BODY:	Be sure to keep your upper body erect, otherwise you cannot execute the throw.
LEGS:	You may possibly step forward here, to shorten the measure.

Step 2	
ARMS:	With your forte against the opponent's neck, throw him backward over your leg.
BODY:	It is important to remain upright and allow the force to come from the upper body.
LEGS:	With your left leg, step behind the left leg of your opponent and then throw him.

If the female fighter is in a weak bind, then the male fighter comes behind her blade with his blade …

… and places his short edge against the female fighter's neck.

Then he throws her over his hip.

THE BREAK AGAINST THE STRIKE-AROUND

The attacker strikes a Cross Strike and the defender parries it.

The attacker then Strikes Around with another Cross Strike.

Step 1	
ARMS:	If your opponent parries the Cross Strike, then strike around with another Cross Strike to the other side. Continue striking Cross Strikes at the upper and lower openings until you hit.
LEGS:	Be sure to step out of line with every Cross Strike.

Step 2	
ARMS:	If your opponent attacks with a Cross Strike which you parry, then he will probably strike around with another Cross Strike. Then simply make a Cross Strike beneath his. Be sure that you have a hanging point and that your hilt covers your head, in case he tries to withdraw with an over-cut.
LEGS:	Remain standing, or step slightly to the outside and back.

The defender breaks this attack by likewise striking a Cross Strike under the attacker's Cross Strike.

157

PRACTICAL TIP:
If the attacker approaches the defender, then the attacker strikes with a Cross Strike, alternating between the left and right openings. This will force the defender to parry repeatedly. As a result, he will become less precise and can ultimately be easily overcome. You should, however, strike around three to four times at most, otherwise the defender will eventually make an adjustment. You can also strike the Cross Strike to the Ox and Plow alternately.

Strike the Cross Strike to the Plow position.

Then strike around to the other side with another Cross Strike to the Ox position, ...

PRACTICAL TIPS

Step 1

ARMS:	Strike a Cross Strike to the Plow position, then strike atound to the other side to the Ox. Alternate three to four times.
LEGS:	Stay in a stable stance. The easiest way may be to perform small jumps as you strike back and forth.

Step 2

ARMS	If your opponent resists your attacks, withdraw with a Crown Strike.

… and strike around again with a Cross Strike to the Ox position.

Then cut across again to the Plow position. Step out of line each time you strike a Cross Strike.

In the end, withdraw with a Crown Strike.

Swordfighting Equipment:
The Hardware

The equipment used in modern swordfighting depends very much on the fighter's approach. Thanks to modern materials, we have a wide choice of possibilities available to us. Swordfighting is, however, not a mass sport, which means that we must "borrow" some of our equipment from other kinds of sport and modify it. Let us begin with the most important piece of sword fighting equipment: the sword.

17.1 The Sword

In choosing the correct sword, the first important consideration is what will be it used for? Is it for training, free fighting or cutting tests? Training swords can be made of wood, bamboo, aluminum or steel. Each material has its advantages and disadvantages.

BAMBOO:
Bamboo swords or so-called shinais come from Japanese kendo. We must modify them somewhat for our purposes, for the original shinais have no cross guard and are also too light. Therefore we must weigh down the shinai with some lead and in this way try to achieve rather more realistic handling.

Shinais are flexible and bend easily on hitting the target. They are, however, too rigid for a massive thrust, as they have almost no give. The design of the shinai causes it to absorb energy when struck. This makes it especially well-suited for free fighting.

Shinais are of limited use in training and many techniques are difficult or even impossible to execute with them. As well, shinais can be broken very easily. Regular maintenance of course helps, but this requires disassembly, which is not everyone's cup of tea. For many fighters, therefore, shinais are a training device with a limited life.

WOOD:
Wooden swords are less expensive to procure and maintain. They have a very wide striking edge and a thick, round tip, which minimizes the risk of injury. Depending on how they are made, maintained and uses, wooden swords can last for a very long time. Unfortunately it is impossible to practice many techniques realistically with wooden swords. They distort the feeling in a Bind and in several techniques. Wooden swords almost never have the balance and weight of good steel swords.

Nevertheless wooden swords can be recommended for beginners. But never underestimate the danger of wooden swords! They are rigid in the thrust and the fighter can easily break any bone with a wooden sword. Wooden swords are therefore not suitable for free fighting.

ALUMINUM:
Aluminum swords are the next step on the path to the proper sword. They are made of metal, which enables many techniques that are difficult to execute with bamboo or wooden swords, such as many techniques from the Bind. Aluminum swords have a wide striking edge. Because of their lighter weight they are somewhat safer than steel swords. But they don't bend in the thrust, which is a major disadvantage. They are thus too dangerous for free fighting and represent an interim solution.

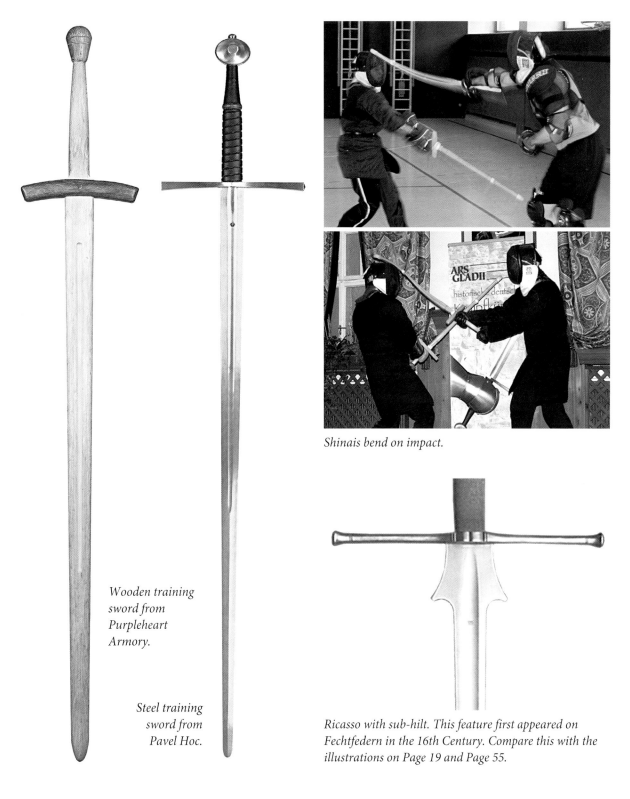

Shinais bend on impact.

Wooden training sword from Purpleheart Armory.

Steel training sword from Pavel Hoc.

Ricasso with sub-hilt. This feature first appeared on Fechtfedern in the 16th Century. Compare this with the illustrations on Page 19 and Page 55.

STEEL:

The blunt steel sword is the best variant. Ideally it has a striking edge with a thickness of at least two millimeters. Balance and weight distribution should be as authentic as possible. If possible, its weight, balance and dimensions should be no different than those of a good, sharp sword. With a steel sword one can fight without limitations, and all techniques can be learned cleanly and precisely. If a steel sword is also used in free fighting, one must be sure that it bends sufficiently in the thrust.

An alternative to regular steel swords are so-called *Fechtfedern*, or practice swords. These are special training swords as used in the 16th century. They bend easily when thrust and almost always have a ricasso, or unsharpened length of blade, in front of the cross guard. When buying a *Fechtfeder*, it is important to be sure that it is not too flexible and if possible does not bend in the blade's forte. Otherwise techniques such as Winding are not possible. This, of course, also applies to steel swords that are to be used in free fighting.

SYNTHETIC MATERIALS:

Synthetic swords offer a cheap and relatively safe alternative to steel. They tend, however, to be whippy, and are therefore unrealistic. The bind is especially affected. Proper transformation of information via the blade is reduced. For delicate work, the synthetic swords are, in my opinion, inferior.

17.2 Protective Gear

Suitable protective gear is indispensible for free fighting. There are hundreds of possibilities here, and each fighter should choose what is best for him. The head, neck, joints, torso, genitals, legs and hands should all be protected.

A metal gorget provides maximum throat protection.

A fencing mask. The fencing mask should be suitable for use with swords. Do not skimp on quality here.

When using a steel sword for free fighting, one should be absolutely sure that it bends when a thrust lands.

Metal arm guards.

Steel sword by Albion, which is suitable for free fighting. It flexes well when thrust—see right.

Protectors made of synthetic material from motocross sport.

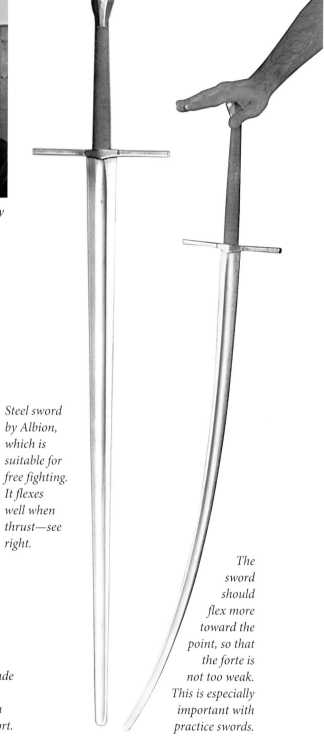

The sword should flex more toward the point, so that the forte is not too weak. This is especially important with practice swords.

163

HEAD:
The head is best protected with a fencing mask, although they usually offer no protection on the back. It is advisable to add something there yourself.

NECK:
Here a steel gorget can be recommended. Even thrusts against the larynx are no problem when wearing one. A good gorget also offers protection against blows on the side of the neck. The bib in front is also important, so that thrusts from below cannot slide under the neck protector. Along with the fencing mask, the gorget is one of the most important pieces of protective gear.

JOINTS:
There are many possible ways to protect elbow, shoulder and knee joints. Suitable protection can be obtained from ice hockey or motocross specialty stores, or try other types of sports protective equipment.

TORSO:
The gambeson has proved most effective in protecting this area. This heavily padded jacket was also used in the Middle Ages. There are fencing jackets available that have been designed specifically for historical fencers and that offer good movement and protection. Those who wish to can also procure breast and shoulder protectors. Several companies offer good protective equipment for riot control.

HANDS:
Heavy gloves for hockey or lacrosse have now become standard. Somewhat cheaper, but still very good, are real fencing gloves.

ADDITIONAL EQUIPMENT:
Underarm protectors, shin guards and a groin protector are definitely recommended.

Of course items of equipment made by a weapons smith are historically correct. Pay attention to both the quality and fit. A piece of equipment is not a hindrance in combat only if it fits well.

Ice hockey gloves for free fighting.

Leather gloves for training. Of course these gloves do not offer adequate protection against injury when free fighting.

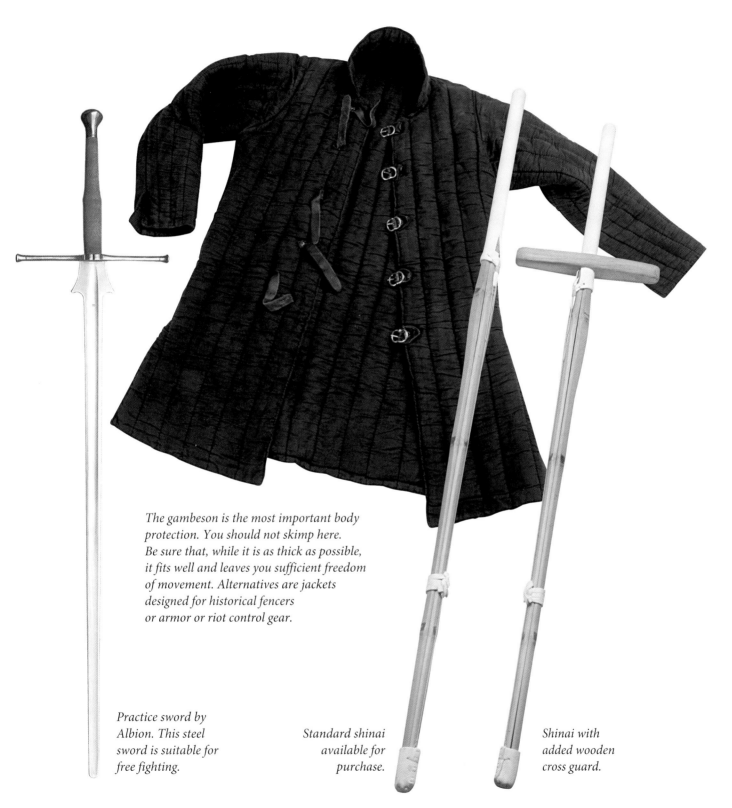

The gambeson is the most important body protection. You should not skimp here. Be sure that, while it is as thick as possible, it fits well and leaves you sufficient freedom of movement. Alternatives are jackets designed for historical fencers or armor or riot control gear.

Practice sword by Albion. This steel sword is suitable for free fighting.

Standard shinai available for purchase.

Shinai with added wooden cross guard.

The Free Fight: Man against Man

The free fight is a very important part of training. Without the free fight, one cannot learn fencing. In free fighting, techniques and one's own skill are put to the test. In free fighting we are repeatedly faced with problems we face in serious fencing. Noted weaknesses should be tackled regularly in free fighting in order to improve. The free fight is the closest thing to real combat with sharp blades.

Today we must consider many things. The risk of damaged joints, broken bones and other serious injuries must be minimized to the extent possible. This is only possible if two things are taken into consideration: equipment and control in combat.

The better the equipment, the less the risk of injury. The less the risk of injury, the greater the fighter's willingness to take risks in combat that he would not take with sharp weapons in real combat. There is the danger that too much protective gear will cause a fighter to lose respect for the blade and become careless. For this reason, only as much protective gear as needed should be used, but not more. As the fencing masters taught long ago: "*Was zehrt, das Lehrt*," which can be loosely translated as "that which hurts, teaches" or "no pain, no gain."

Apart from the protective gear worn, one's own weapon must be kept under control at all times. If you are too tired or too distracted to have sufficient concentration and control in a combat, then stop it immediately. This is not only better for you, but also fair to your partner. Blows should be struck with full speed in free fighting, but not necessarily with full force. As well, you should be able to stop a strike or thrust if you see that your partner will be injured by it. With sufficient training, much can be done for safety in this respect. Never forget: it is about training and learning, not winning. You are fighting with a partner and not an opponent!

In free fighting one tries to defeat the opponent. All of the techniques come into use, but also footwork, strikes and throws. The goal is to simulate a serious sword fight, as safely but also as realistically as possible. Safety is the number one rule – but nevertheless the opponent's every weakness is exploited, in order to decide the combat in your favor. You should also begin a free fight with this attitude.

For this reason, before combat it is important to clarify what this combat is all about. For this reason, I have established the following stages of training:

- Technique training
- Technique combat
- Training combat
- Free fighting

You will find more on this in Chapter 20.

With the proper equipment, even free fighting is a safe activity.

The Crown in a free fight. In this situation, balance often determines subsequent possibilities.

The fighter on the left has executed an under-cut, positioning himself for a thrust.

Leaving the line of attack results in many possibilities.

Under-cut beneath an over-cut. Footwork and measure are decisive here.

Tested in a free fight: zero-in the point or strike a Strike of Wrath over the Bind.

It is enough not to be where the opponent strikes. Avoiding is better than parrying.

If the line of attack is not closed, then two blows often land as a result.

169

Test Cutting:
Realistic Exercises

In historical European sword fighting, we try to learn and implement the techniques that have been passed down to us as realistically as possible. Ultimately that means that we train for a duel to the death. This also includes learning how to handle a sharp sword properly. This takes place in so-called test cutting.

19.1 Seven Reasons for Test Cutting

Test cutting is extremely important and an integral part of the training program. There are various reasons for this:

SLICE GUIDANCE:
To be able to execute a slice or blow effectively, the blade must be guided cleanly and precisely on the slicing plane. In the best case, the blade is exactly on the slicing plane. This can only be practiced through test cutting. A sharp blade is used, and any deviation is immediately perceptible and visible.

BALANCE / POSTURE:
Cutting through materials is only part of the correct technique. Equally important are the correct tracking with the arms, maintaining balance and sure footwork. After completing a blow you should be in a position to fight off a possible attack, strike a second blow or get out of the way.

ASSESSING EFFECTIVENESS:
Anyone who has never made a test cut with a sharp weapon often underestimates the effectiveness of the techniques. It is also useful to carry out a certain technique or situation as a test cut to test its effectiveness.

RESPECT FOR THE WEAPON:
Anyone who carries out test cuts regularly, has a great deal of respect for a sword. This not only makes training safer, it also allows combat to become more realistic.

EVALUATING THE WEAPON:
The characteristics of the various sword types are best revealed in a test cut. To make a final judgment on a sword, it is always best if one has cut with the sword.

EVALUATING THE FORCE:
Not until test cutting, does one realize how little force is required to effectively slice and strike if the blow is executed cleanly. This provides the stimulus to pay attention to clean blade motion, even in training. It also helps when estimating the necessary force for the various techniques.

SERIOUS STRIKING:
It makes a great difference, whether one is only striking at an opponent in training, if possible without touching him, or whether one strikes a serious, powerful blow. In training, one is accustomed to stopping a blow before reaching, or in the worst case on, the opponent, but in real combat the blow would not end at the opponent. It is impossible to bridge these differences without test cutting.

Cut test with a water-filled plastic bottle: the cleaner the cut the less spray there is.

Cut test with a gourd: gourds allow you to follow the progress of the cut very well.

Overall, test cutting gives one a sense of the effects of a sword, the effectiveness of the techniques and of working with a sharp blade generally. Proper handling of a sharp blade also trains us to evaluate a technique in combat, whether in a friendly training combat or a tournament— our appraisal of a hit will be more realistic.

There is one other reason to conduct regular cutting tests: it is great fun!

19.2 Materials for Cutting Tests

A wide variety of materials are suitable for use in cutting tests:

- Plastic bottles of all sizes
- Beverage cartons (milk, fruit juice, etc.)
- Beverage cans
- Bath mats
- Straw mats
- Tameshigiri mats (Tatami)
- Newspapers
- Cardboard
- Gourds
- Melons

These materials must, however, be prepared for the cut test in different ways:

- Simply fill plastic bottles, beverage cartons and beverage cans with water and if possible close:

- Tightly roll bath mats, straw mats, Tatami and newspapers. In this way it is possible to vary the thickness. Bath mats usually have a cloth edging. This can be folded inward when rolling to that none of the edging is on the outside. Bath mats, Tatami and newspapers have roughly the same cut resistance as muscle tissue, making them very realistic targets. To simulate bones, you can roll freshly-cut branches the width of a finger inside them.

The rolled Tatami or straw mats are tied with twine. If aesthetics are not an issue, you can also simply work with elastic bands. Then the rolls should be soaked in water for several hours (overnight, for example). After soaking, the rolls should be placed upright for an hour or longer to allow excess water to drain.

Newspapers should be soaked briefly so that the paper absorbs the water, but not so long that they begin to dissolve. Take the damp newspapers out of the water and roll them tightly. This will squeeze out the excess water. Secure the rolled newspaper with elastic bands.

- Gourds, melons, heads of cabbage and other vegetables should be as firm as possible. With gourds in particular, be sure that while the skin has a certain firmness it is not completely hardened.

Not recommended are cardboard tubes, branches, old bones, metal plates and the like. The material to cut should be moist if possible.

19.3 Securing the Materials

Different materials are suited for training or simulating different things, therefore you should always work with a variety of materials. The way you secure the cutting material also contributes to the result. Basically there are four different securing methods that are acceptable. Standing and hanging attachments are most common in practice.

Bath mat after being soaked and rolled. Soaking makes the fibers tougher and at the same time more supple, which demands precise blade guidance.

A mat with a piece of a gambeson. This method also allows you to test the effectiveness of this piece of armor.

Severed mat with a fresh branch in the middle. The branch simulates a bone.

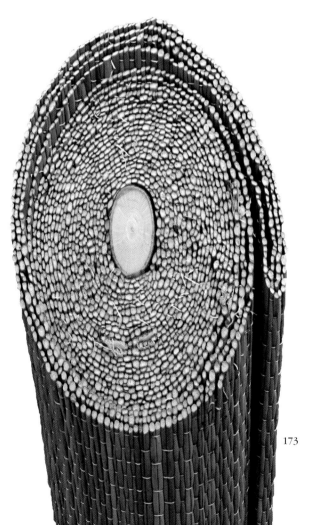

STANDING ATTACHMENT:
Simply place the bottles, cartons or gourds on a post, pedestal or the like. Be sure that you place them at different heights to simulate various body parts. Rolled mats, newspapers and others are best stuck on a small spike. That can be a wooden dowel, a long nail or something else. All that matters is that the spike prevents the long roll from falling over. Rolled mats—especially if they are wet—are seldom well-balanced.

If you sit a plastic bottle on a pedestal and then strike it, you will soon find that the bottle is easily knocked away but will not be severed if your blade guidance is not clean. The worse your blade guidance, the more the undamaged bottle will fly about. Use smaller bottles as your results improve. A two-liter bottle is easier to penetrate than a half-liter one. The severed bottle also allows you to see how clean your cut was. Ideally, the cut should be straight and smooth. Of course the same applies to beverage cartons.

Rolled mats and newspapers behave somewhat differently in this respect. They are also easily knocked off a post or stand. The spike makes them somewhat more stable, and they possess some give. Rolled materials allow you to see the effect of a sword strike very well. Even light blows leave behind an impressive wound provided they are executed cleanly.

HANGING ATTACHMENT:
Cutting bottles, mats or other cutting materials while they are hanging is even more challenging. Even the smallest mistake will cause the target to move out of the way. You will find that the cuts in the material are not as clean as before. The swordsman is in movement, especially in combat. For this reason it is important to practice frequently on suspended targets in order to get a feel for movement. You can also allow the target to swing slowly to simulate movement.

19.4 Tips for the Cutting Test

Start with simple materials. Become familiar with the sword and its swinging behavior. Work your way up from filled plastic bottles to rolled newspapers and bamboo mats (Tatami). Not until you are proficient should you begin adding branches or similar materials into the targets.

You should use the best quality sword that you can find for cutting tests. A good sword costs money, no question. Nevertheless avoid cheap swords, for they are not only dangerous but they also give a false feeling for working with a sharp blade. Instead, pool your resources with a few friends and together buy a good sword. Be sure that the sword is suitable for cutting tests. In the appendix you will find a list of manufacturers which, in my opinion, produce reasonable swords. The sword should also be as sharp as possible. Be sure that it has a fine edge without being too delicate.

When conducting cut tests, be sure that you have a clear view of the surrounding area. It should be clear to everyone what is going on there. Be sure that no children or animals can run into the area of the cut test. Keep a telephone with the emergency number handy. You should also have a first aid kit on hand. Familiarize yourself with the necessary first aid measures. You should never carry out cut tests alone, so that there is someone to help you in the event of an accident. Obviously you should never carry out cut tests if you have been drinking alcohol or have taken medication. Be sure to have good footwear, and change position if water from the targets makes the ground slippery.

A supplement for purists: animal cadavers provide the most realistic results in a cut test. In our society this topic must be addressed sensibly. There are surely many people who feel that using an animal cadaver for cutting tests is inappropriate. On the other hand, animal cadavers are not only burned, they are also ground and used as fertilizer or feed. The reader is free to use whatever he likes for his cut test, but I would like to make a few remarks about the use of animal cadavers:

- Be sure that the animal was killed quickly, painlessly, and with the minimum possible stress.
- Animal cadavers are best hung.
- Cut tests on cadavers are very messy. Put a sheet under the cadaver and wear old clothes.
- Be sure not to disturb anyone. Carry out the cut test where you will not be seen and where no one will feel bothered.
- The cadaver should be as fresh as possible. Bones harden very quickly.
- Decide ahead of time what you will do with the carcass afterward.
- Obey all applicable laws.

You can learn a great deal from test cutting on animal cadavers, but they are not absolutely necessary. The other materials provide equally good results. If in doubt, avoid using cadavers. Every sword fighter is responsible for the reputation of historical sword fighting, and we do not want to damage its reputation for the sake of a few cut tests.

Suspended mat. This type of attachment means that the mat has no resistance. The cut must be executed very cleanly if the mat is to be severed cleanly.

Safety in Training:
The Most Important Point

Sword fighting in the 21st century comes with problems that one must not ignore. Foremost is the question of safety. The sword is a weapon, and even wooden swords and blunt steel swords are dangerous. It is easy to cause serious injuries or even kill someone with them. So how should you train in a martial art designed to kill the opponent, without injuring your partner? Everyone involved in sword fighting faces this problem.

There are several approaches in meeting this requirement. Basically the problem can be approached on two paths: training and equipment.

20.1 Safety through Proper Training

Most important is control of your weapon and your own body. From early on, therefore, exercises should be carried out with the goal of improving control of the weapon. These include stop blows, which means striking every possible type of blow at a target without touching it. Stop blows also offer you many tactical advantages in combat—just think of the "*Fehler.*" Good balance and posture during training enables us to have good control in combat.

You must be able to trust your partner. You should only go as far in training or combat as you can trust your partner. If you see that the combat is overwhelming your partner, stop immediately. Such signs could include:

- Fatigue, recognizable by footwork difficulties, heavy breathing and lack of control over the weapon.

- Footwork mistakes, sagging of the legs.

- Wild flailing or rigid blocks that only serve to stop the opponent's weapon.

Concentration is always a requirement when training. Clear rules help avoid misunderstandings. The training partners should salute before a combat or training session to indicate that they are ready. This can be done by raising the sword, for example. The signal to end the combat should be just as clear. It is best to indicate it both verbally (shout "Halt," "Stop" or "Out") and visually (for example raising the empty hand).

More injuries occur while fooling around than in actual training. Flailing about playfully very quickly leads to accidents, because you are neither concentrating nor following any rules. Fooling around often happens when you are tired, which represents an added risk. Never forget: accidents with swords, even wooden ones, can have fatal consequences!

20.2 Structure of Training

The following sequence is useful for learning new techniques:

- technique training
- technique combat
- training combat
- free fighting

TECHNIQUE TRAINING:

Here a technique is practiced slowly, in order to learn a movement. It is clear who is to carry out the technique and also what the partner is to do. Speed can be increased as confidence grows.

TECHNIQUE COMBAT:

Here the technique is practiced in an open environment. The partner has several opportunities to attack and can work on both timing and measure. Technique combat is usually carried out at half speed or even slower. It is clear

who is attacking and who is executing the technique. There is a stop after one or two executions. The combat is then analyzed and discussed. The one carrying out the technique being practiced determines the duration, tempo and intensity level of the combat. He gives instructions which his training partner follows.

TRAINING COMBAT:

The purpose here is to clarify a certain principle or question. That can have complex contexts or be a simple question that can only be answered in practice. Training combat is only slightly slower than actual combat. Both fighters must be in absolute control. The object is not winning, rather giving the partner the opportunity to train. The two fighters therefore adhere as closely as possible to the training theme. Usually it is decided who will be the attacker and who will defend. This can change during the combat. The same sequence is often practiced over and over again, until, for example, a mistake is recognized or a problem solves itself.

Wooden swords are used when learning individual techniques.

FREE FIGHTING:

The object here is to defeat the opponent. Everything is permitted and nothing is excluded. Obviously the safety of the training partner must be assured. On the other hand there are no rules. Here and only here, all of the opponent's weaknesses are exploited and everything possible is used to defeat him. One's own mistakes become clearest in unrestricted free fighting. The stress created in such a combat helps make it even more difficult. The psychological demands of combat also become most evident in free fighting.

20.3 Safety through Proper Equipment

Good protective gear should always be worn. When free fighting with shinais, attention must be paid to thrusts. Because shinais bend little in a thrust, serious injuries can result if too much force or resistance is used. It is especially dangerous if a fighter runs or leaps into a thrust.

A beginner should only train with a wooden or bamboo sword (shinai), which reduce the risk of injury. As control and responsibility improve, one can also begin practicing with steel or aluminum swords. Another possibility is the co-called "Federschwert." They are very flexible and allow for thrusting in a fight.

If both fighters are in a strong Bind, they often end up in the Crown.

If you are using a suitable steel sword, then the thrust is not so much a problem as steel swords flex. You should, however, be concerned about the strike. With a steel sword you can easily break any bone, even through a gambeson. Be sure not to use more force than necessary and possibly catch it slightly before it lands. It is up to the fighter himself to find an acceptable balance between safety and realism.

With steel swords in particular, be sure to purchase a lighter rather than heavier weapon. You should be careful with any sword that weighs more than 1600 grams (3.5 pounds). While a well-made sword can easily weigh more than 1600 grams, these are usually the exception rather than the rule.

Always wear gloves when training. Leather forearm protectors are also advisable, especially if you are technique training, where you work on the opponent's forearms (slicing off, etc.). A fencing mask is a must, even if there is only a remote possibility of the head being struck, which is all the time. Partners who work well together can perhaps train with steel swords without protective gear, but it is not advisable. At the very least, a fencing mask should always be worn.

All other items of equipment, such as gambesons, elbow, knee and shin protectors, shin guards, forearm protectors, gorgets and heavy gloves, are actually only needed for free fighting or when you are practicing a specific technique in which your sword makes contact.

A fighter in free fighting equipment: fencing mask, gorget, gambeson, hockey gloves. One can also wear forearm protectors, elbow guards and shin or knee protectors.

Practical
Training Tips

In the course of training you will always encounter things that you should consider and which repeatedly cause problems. Here are several tips that can make your training more effective.

GUARDS

Regularly carry out a guard sequence, in which you assume all of the guard positions and continually change between them. This will make you familiar with all the guards, and in time the postures will become quite natural. Always stay in the selected guard for a while and try to be relaxed but not lax. "Ready to react, but not tensed" is the goal of this exercise.

Then, while remaining very relaxed, execute every possible attack from each guard. Get used to attacking from a wide variety of angles from each guard. During this exercise pay attention to proper footwork, balance, and above all, clean blade guidance. You should be capable of starting even unconventional attacks from every guard.

BLOWS

Practice the Master Strikes as frequently as possible, as well as over- and under-cuts. You should strive to make every blow as perfect as possible. This includes clean blade guidance as well as good balance while striking and transferring power from body rotation to the blow. Very little striking power comes from the arms; the majority originates from the body.

Train to make double strikes, by striking through on one side and then striking from the associated hang from the other side. You should be capable of striking every blow from a hang.

Practice stop blows. These are blows that are directed at a target with maximum speed and force, but without striking the target. You halt the blow just before the target. This gives you great certainty in handling your weapon and makes training safer for your partner.

THRUSTS

Do not ignore thrusts. Bring your entire body into play when making a thrust. Practice executing the thrust as quickly as possible from a great distance. Your thrust should be quick and surprising, but under control.

LEFT, RIGHT

Practice every strike, every guard, every technique both from the left and right. As a right-hander, you should pay more attention to your left side. In the end, it should not matter to you whether you execute it from the left or right. You can practice this every day, consciously using your left hand more.

BLADE FOLLOW-UP

When technique training, the combatant who is struck should always continue wielding his blade. In the real thing, a fighter will not always stop a hand or arm movement just because he is struck. This follow-up forces the fighter to pay attention to his own cover and respect the opponent's blade. By doing so you will immediately see whether the respective lines of attack were covered or not.

FOOTWORK

Footwork is extremely important. Though it is different for each person, it is important that every fighter always have a stable posture from which he can act and generate force at any time.

LINE OF VISION

You should practice a "peripheral vision," seeing and perceiving as much as possible from the corners of the eyes. Look your opponent straight in the face, in the eyes. At the same time you should also keep his shoulders in sight. Never look at the opponent's weapon, or even worse, at the point of his weapon.

MEASURE

Make every attack, every strike, so that it can land. If you strike past the opponent in training, then not only are you fighting unrealistically, you are depriving your partner of the opportunity to learn the techniques properly.

SPEED

Work slowly. At the start consciously do everything very slowly. Learn the correct movements first. Soon they will become second nature, and it will be easy to increase speed. It is important to learn to execute movements cleanly, so that under stress they can be recalled again cleanly. This point is often overlooked.

ERRORS IN TECHNIQUE

If a technique does not work, then repeat it until it does. If you cannot reach the point where the technique works, then work on interpreting the technique. You can assume that the historical techniques handed down to us are correct. The mistake usually lies with oneself, therefore always begin there.

CLEAR INTENTIONS

Tell your training partner as clearly as possible what you want to practice, how fast and how intensely. The objective should always be clear.

PASSIVE PARTNER

The training partner, who is the recipient of the technique and usually "dies" in the end, should take his role seriously. Make clean attacks, exert some force in the Bind and alert your partner to poor balance, incorrect footwork or other errors. At this moment you take on the role of a control mechanism and you have to assess whether the technique has functioned. Good training is only possible with a good partner.

FOOLING AROUND

The temptation to fool around with the sword is great. Make yourself aware that most accidents occur in this situation.

PRACTICE FREQUENCY

Practice as often as possible, even if it is for only five minutes, during which you strike several blows.

PLAYING ALLOWED

Play with your weapon—with the necessary caution. Take the sword in your hands as often as possible. Become familiar with its weight, its handling, its length. The more familiar you are with the weapon the better.

RESULTS ORIENTATION

Pay attention to what you are training. You will be able to do what you train for, therefore you should repeatedly check whether you are still on the path that you actually want to follow. That is particularly important in free fighting, in order not to become "routine blinded."

CHECKS BY A THIRD PERSON

Ask a third training partner to observe your free fight. Not only will you receive useful feedback, but this third person will also be able to confirm that you do not exceed the previously determined speed. That is another safety aspect. It is also always helpful to record the engagements with a video camera.

Links

**FIGHTING SCHOOLS AND
SERIOUS SWORDFIGHTING GROUPS:**

EUROPE:
HEMAC — www.hemac.org

AUSTRIA:
Ars Gladii — www.arsgladii.at
Dreynschlag — www.dreynschlag.at
Fachverband für
historisches Fechten — www.historisches-fechten.at
Klingenspiel — www.klingenspiel.at
Rittersporn — www.rittersporn.at

GERMANY:
Ochs — www.schwertkampf-ochs.de
Zornhau — www.zornhau.de
Freifechter — www.freifechter.de
Hammaborg — www.hammaborg.de

SWITZERLAND:
Freywild — www.freywild.ch

ENGLAND:

Schola Gladiatoria — www.fioredeiliberi.org
Boars Tooth — www.boarstooth.org

FRANCE:
De Taille et d'Estoc — www.detailleetdestoc.com

*Other groups in Europe can be found on the map by
Ars Gladii. Simply look under the heading "Links" at
www.arsgladii.at. This map is updated regularly.*

Internet Forums

ARS GLADII FORUM:
www.forum.arsgladii.at or on the homepage
of Ars Gladii

SCHOLA GLADIATORIA FORUM:
www.fioredeiliberi.org/phpBB2/index.php

Swords and Equipment

The following is only a small selection
of current manufacturers.

STEEL TRAINING SWORDS:
Albion — www.albion-europe.com
or www.albion-swords.com

Pavel Moc — www.swords.cz

Paul Chen — www.casiberia.com

SHARP SWORDS:
Albion — www.albion-europe.com
or www.albion-swords.com

Bibliography

ALBRECHT DÜRER'S FENCING BOOK HS. 26-232 / ALBERTINA
(Graphic Collection),
Wien
Cod. 1246 / University
Library
Breslau

CGM 558
Translation by
Didier de Grenier,
Michael Huber and
Phillipe Errard

COD. HS. 3227A
Translation by David
Lindholm

COD. 1074 NOVI BY WOLFENBÜTTEL
Translation by
Alexander Kiermayer

CODEX WALLERSTEIN
Grzegorz Zabinski and
Bartlomiej Walczak
ISBN: 1-58160-339-8
Paladin Press

THE SWORD
Thomas Laible
ISBN: 978-3-38711-05-7
Wieland Verlag

GERMAN BLADE ARCHIVES
Heinz Huther
Self-published

EGENOLPH 1529
Translation by
Alexander Kiermayer

GLADIATORIA KK5013 / MS. GERM. QUART 16 / COD. GUELF. 78.2 AUG 2°
Translation by
Carsten Lorbeer,
Pragmatic literacy

HANS VON SPEYER
M.I.29 University
Library
Salzburg

HS.BEST.7020
Historical Archive of
Cologne
Translation by Andreas
Meier, Marita Wiedner,
Pragmatic literacy

JAKOB SUTOR'S ARTIFICIAL FENCING BOOK
ISBN: 3-937188-26-6
VRZ Verlag

JOURNAL OF THE ARMOUR RESEARCH SOCIETY
Volume 1, 2005
ISSN 1557-1297
Armour Research
Society

JUDE LEW COD. I.6.4°. 3
University Library
Salzburg, Translation
by Grzegorz Zabinski

MEISTER JOHANNES LIECHTENAUERS ART OF FENCING
Martin Wierschin
C.H. Beck Verlag,
München

P 5126 (incomplete
copy, late 15th century)
Kunsthistorisches
Museum
Wien, Ms. Chart.
B1021, 1542 / Research
Library
Gotha,
Castle Friedenstein

PAULUS HECTOR MAIR
Codex Vindobonensis
Palatinus 10.825
Österr. National Library
/ Wien

PAULUS KAL CGM 1507, CA. 1460
The Bavarian
State Library
München

PETER VON DANZIG COD. 44 A 8 (COD. 1449) 1452
Bibliotheca
dell'Academica
Nazinale dei Lincei
and Corsiniana
Translation by
Grzegorz Zabinski

RECORDS OF THE MEDIEVAL SWORD
Ewart Oakeshott
ISBN: 0-85115-566-9
Boydell & Brewer LTD

SIGMAND RINGECK MSCR. DRESD. C487
Saxon State Library
/ Dresden
Translation by Martin
Wierschin

SOLOTHURNER FECHTBUCH
1506 - 1514
Zentralbibliothek
Solothurn

SWORDS OF THE VIKING AGE
Ian Peirce
ISBN: 1-84383-089-2
Boydell Press

THE MARTIAL ARTS OF RENAISSANCE EUROPE
Sydney Anglo
ISBN: 0-300-08352-1
Yale University Press

THE MEDIEVAL ART OF SWORDSMANSHIP
Jeffrey L. Forgeng
ISBN: 1-891448-38-2
Chivalry Bookshelf

THE SECRET HISTORYOF THE SWORD
J. Christoph Amberger
ISBN: 1-892515-04-0
Multi-Media Books

THE SWORD IN THE AGE OF CHIVALRY
Ewart Oakeshott
ISBN: 0-85115-362-3
Boydell Press

STRANGLEHOLD AND DEATH BLOW
Hans Czynner
Ute Bergner and
Johannes Giessauf
ISBN: 10-3-201-01855-4
Adeva Verlag

GLOSSARY (*German terms*)

A

Abnehmen
To move away or free yourself from a bind or begin an attack from a bind.

Abreissen
To follow the opponent's weapon or hands, usually with the hilt downward. Push the opponent's weapon or hands down with the hilt.

Abschneiden (Slice Off)
To slice across the opponent's hands from below or above.

Abschnappen (Snap Off)
To disengage from a bind by sliding or batting the blade away with a strong blow.

Absetzen (Set Aside)
To simultaneously parry the opponent's blade while making a thrust—usually from the Ox or Plow.

Abziehen (Withdraw)
To disengage from the opponent and move out of range of his weapon. Usually after the combat has ended.

Alber (Fool)
One of the six guards. The sword is held downward, the point is held in front of you pointing diagonally at the ground.

Am Schwert (On the Sword)
To execute an attack from a bind. You work "on the sword."

Anbinden (Crossing of the Blades)
The engaged position with weapons crossed, in which the weapons come together at the moment of contact. A distinction is made between "being hard on the sword" or "soft on the sword."

Ansetzen (Place)
An attack aimed at a certain body part.

B

Band (Bind)
The moment of contact between two weapons and the actual contact of two weapons.

Blösse (Openings)
The opponent's four openings. The first is his right side above the belt, the second is his left above the belt, the third is his right side below the belt and the fourth is his left below the belt. Also called Fenster (Windows).

Brentschirn
A state of "battle" in which the edges of the swords rub together in the binding position. From this position you try to take the opponent's sword.

Bruch (Break)
The counter to a certain technique. The break foils a technique.

Buckler
Small round hand shield, also called a fist shield.

Büffel (Buffalo)
Disparaging term for a fighter who relies solely on his strength and aggression.

D

Drei Häue (Three Blows)
Three blows in succession—an under-cut from the right, an under-cut from the left, followed by a powerful Crown Strike.

Drei Wunder (Three Wonders)
The three components of sword fighting: the cut, the thrust and the slice.

Duplieren (Doubling)
To strike the opponent from a binding position. Your own blade often comes between the opponent's sword and the opponent, making a defense almost impossible.

Durchlaufen (Running Through)
The attempt to pass the opponent's weapon and reach his back.

G

Durchsetzen (Push Through)
A timed thrust whose target is between the opponent's hands and body.

Durchstreichen (Striking Through)
To carry through a blow from below against the opponent's blade to the point that you separate from the bind and thrust at another opening.

Durchwechseln (Changing Through)
Avoiding contact with the opponent's blade and seeking another opening, usually with a thrust from the Ox. Can also happen from a bind.

Gehilz (Hilt)
The grip of the sword including cross guard, grip and pommel. Gehilz also sometimes refers to the cross guard.

Geschränkter Ort
A thrust, in which the hands are held crossed over, the left hand under right.

Gewappnet Stehen
A stance where the sword becomes a barrier in front of the body, with the left hand grasping the middle of the blade and the hilt in the right hand.

E

Einhorn (Unicorn)
The Unicorn is an end position after an under-cut, with the point aimed high. In the right Unicorn the arms are crossed.

Einlaufen (Running In)
To change from a near to a close measure. Usually followed by wrestling and/or throws. Running In is the beginning of wrestling on the sword.

Eisenpforte (Iron Gate)
A guard in which the point is placed on the ground in front of you. Similar to the Barrier or Fool Guard.

H

Halbschwert (Half-Sword)
A technique in which you grip your sword with the left hand in order to achieve a more precise thrust. Used mainly in armed combat.

Handarbeit (Handwork)
The combat itself—between the approach and withdrawal. The actual sword fight occurs during Handwork.

Hängen (Hanging)
Stance in which the point or the pommel "hangs" downward.

F

Fehler (Feint)
A feint. It is carried out as if you are about to attack a certain opening, in order to attack another vulnerable opening.

Fläche (Flat)
The flat, or broad side, of the blade.

Fühlen (To Feel)
While in a binding position, to sense whether the enemy is hard or soft in the bind. Sense his intentions.

Hängetort (Hanging Point)
Position in which the point hangs downward. The hilt is held over the head. If you are in a right Hanging Point, the point hangs down to the left.

Huten (Guards)
The basic stances. According to Liechtenauer there are four different guards, while Ringeck names six. They are: Fool, Plow, Ox, From the Roof, Barrier and Tail Guards. In many combat manuals there are even more, however most are variations of Ringeck's six basic guards.

I

Indes (Meanwhile)
Not "Before" or "After," but "Meanwhile" or "at the same time." Most important tempo in sword fighting, because it is the only safe one.

K

Krauthacke (Garden Hoe)
A swift sequence of vertical blows to the upper and lower openings, during which you step toward the opponent.

Kreuz (Cross)
The cross formed by the cross guard and the blade. Sometimes also a synonym for cross guard.

Krieg (War)
Winding, mutating, doubling, binding etc.—all the techniques that take place at relatively close quarters. The point is mainly used in the War position.

Kron (Crown)
Defensive technique in which you lift your sword and deflect the opponent's blade with your cross guard or forte.

Krumphau (Crooked Strike)
Technique in which the arms are crossed, for example countering an over-cut with the short edge from a right Plow and ending in a left Plow. When executing a Crooked Strike you step toward the opponent with a cross step.

Kurze Schneide (Short Edge)
Also called the "false edge." The edge of the sword that normally points toward the fighter when holding the sword normally in front of him.

L

Lange Schneide (Long Edge)
The edge of the sword that strikes the target in a normal blow. The edge that points away from the fighter when holding the sword normally in front of him.

Langort (Long Point)
Also called "Long Guard." An additional guard, with the blade horizontal and the arms extended straight forward. The hands and blade form a line.

Leger/Läger (Position)
To assume a position.

Leichmeister (Dance Master)
Dance master, especially for arms-dance and arms-plays. A derogatory term.

Linke Klinge
Short edge.

M

Meisterhau (Master Strike)
According to Ringeck there are five Master Strikes: Crooked Strike, Strike of Wrath, Cross Strike, Crown Strike and Squinting Strike.

Mensur (Measure)
Distance. The term refers to the various distances between fighters during combat.

Mittelhau (Middle-Cut)
A left-to-right horizontal side cut at medium height.

Mordschlag (Death Blow)
A technique in which you hold the blade with both hands and strike with the hilt.

Mordstück (Death Maneuver)
A maneuver which ends in the death of one or both fighters.

Mutieren (Mutate)
A Winding technique in which you thrust from the Ox position past the opponent's hands to his lower openings without losing blade contact.

N

Nach (After)
When the opponent attacks, you end up in the "After" (by merely parrying). In the "After" you only react to the opponent.

Natternzunge (Viper Tongue)
A rapidly-repeated sequence of thrusts over the opponent's hilt, during which a changing through movement is repeatedly indicated but never carried out, until the opponent becomes confused and leaves an opening for a thrust. The movement resembles the flicking tongue of a viper.

Nebenhut (Tail Guard)
One of the six guards. The sword is held with the cross guard at hip level, the point is aimed down and back.

O

Ochs (Ox)
One of the six guards. The sword is held with the cross guard at eye level or higher, the point aimed at the opponent's face. Optimally place the thumb on the blade.

Oberhau (Over-Cut)
Every blow that is struck from above.

Ort (Point)
The tip of the sword.

P

Pflug (Plow)
One of the six guards. The sword is held with the grip at hip level, the point is aimed up and forward, toward the opponent.

R

Rauschen (Swoosh)
To attack with a rapid succession of blows.

Redel (Wheel)
To hold the sword with an outstretched right arm and execute a swift circular-motion of the blade in front.

S

Scheitelhau (Crown Strike)
One of the Master Strikes. A vertical downward blow, from the "crown."

Schielhau (Squinting Strike)
One of the Master Strikes. A downward cut with the short edge at the opponent's shoulder or neck.

Schlüssel (Key)
A guard in which the hilt is held far back. The blade rests on the left arm, pointing forward. The hilt is held roughly in front of the right breast.

Schrankhut (Barrier Guard)
One of the six guards. The sword is held in front of you, with the point aimed at the ground. The Barrier can be executed with the blade held vertically or diagonally in front of you.

Schwäche (Foible)
The first third of the blade, beginning at the point and extending to the middle.

Schnappen (Snap)
To execute a sudden movement of the blade from the bind and immediately strike the side of the opponent's blade. During the movement the pommel snaps forward and back.

Sprechfenster (Talking Window)
The blades are in a strong bind, and you wait for or determine the opponent's intentions.

Stärke (Forte)
The last third of the blade from the cross guard to the middle.

Streichen (Cancel)
To direct a blow from below against the opponent's blade to cancel their action.

Stücke (Device)
Also known as a "fighting trick." Techniques or attack combinations designed to get past an opponent's defenses.

Sturzhau (Plunging Cut)
A powerful strike, in which you advance and simultaneously strike from above with the short edge with crossed hands.

U

Überlaufen (Overrunning)
A blow which reaches the opponent before his reaches you. For example a Crown Strike against the legs.

Umschlagen (Strike Around)
To pull away after a blow for another to the opposite side.

Unterhau (Under-Cut)
Every blow that is struck from below.

V

Verkehrer
A technique in which, from a strong bind, the opponent is thrown with the help of his elbow.

Versatzungen (Displacements)
There are four Displacements and they describe the breaks for the four basic guards: Crooked Strike breaks Ox, Crown Strike breaks Fool, Cross Strike breaks From the Roof, Squinting Strike breaks Plow.

Versetzen (Displace)
Deflect an attack with your own attack/blow, so that it misses its target.

Verzucken (Twitch)
Suddenly and abruptly change the direction of attack.

Vom Tag (From the Roof)
One of the six guards. The sword is held with the cross guard at chin height or over the head. The point is aimed upward or slightly to the rear.

Vor (Before)
If you are fighting in the "Before," then you retain the initiative and the opponent reacts to your attacks.

W

Wechsel (Change)
A guard similar to the Tail Guard, with the long edge facing down.

Wechselhau (Changing Cut)
If a strike misses and you withdraw the blade along the same attacking plane in order to strike with the short edge, it is called a Changing Cut.

Weckmeister
A upward thrust at the opponent's face, made after an attack from the Plow has been parried.

Winden (Winding)
Any turning of the blade while pressing on the opponent's blade in order to bring one end or the other of your sword (point or pommel) against him. There is a total of 24 Winds (1 x 2 x 3 x 4 + 24)" "One winding from two sides with three attacks to the four openings."

Z

Zecken (Tick)
A light strike with the weapon.

Zornhau (Strike of Wrath)
One of the Master Strikes. An over-cut that is struck with great force, either from the right or from above

Zucken (Drawing)
An abrupt disengagement from the bind, downward and to the rear, immediately followed by a thrust. Can also be executed without binding.

Zufechten (Approach)
The part of the combat before you reach striking distance. In the approach neither opponent can reach the other with his word.

Zwerchhau (Cross Strike)
One of the Master Strikes A blow that is struck more or less on the horizontal plane (from the side), in contrast to an over-cut, for example. The Cross Strike is not a middle-cut.

GLOSSARY (*English terms*)

A

After
When the opponent attacks, you end up in the "After" (by merely parrying). In the "After" you only react to the opponent.

B

Barrier Guard
One of the six guards. The sword is held in front of you, with the point aimed at the ground. The Barrier can be executed with the blade held vertically or diagonally in front of you.

Before
If you are fighting in the "Before," then you retain the initiative and the opponent reacts to your attacks.

Bind
The moment of contact between two weapons and the actual contact of two weapons.

Break
The counter to a certain technique. The break foils a technique.

Buckler
Small round hand shield, also called a fist shield.

Buffalo
Disparaging term for a fighter who relies solely on his strength and aggression.

C

Cancel
To direct a blow from below against the opponent's blade to cancel their action.

Change
A guard similar to the Tail Guard, with the long edge facing down.

Changing Cut
If a strike misses and you withdraw the blade along the same attacking plane in order to strike with the short edge, it is called a Changing Cut.

Changing Through
Avoiding contact with the opponent's blade and seeking another opening, usually with a thrust from the Ox. Can also happen from a bind.

Crooked Strike
Technique in which the arms are crossed, for example countering an over-cut with the short edge from a right Plow and ending in a left Plow. When executing a Crooked Strike you step toward the opponent with a cross step.

Cross
The cross formed by the cross guard and the blade. Sometimes also a synonym for cross guard.

Crossing of the Blades
The engaged position with weapons crossed, in which the weapons come together at the moment of contact. A distinction is made between "being hard on the sword" or "soft on the sword."

Crown
Defensive technique in which you lift your sword and deflect the opponent's blade with your cross guard or forte.

Crown Strike
One of the Master Strikes. A vertical downward blow, from the "crown."

D

Death Blow
A technique in which you hold the blade with both hands and strike with the hilt.

Death Device
A device which ends in the death of one or both fighters.

Device
Also known as a "fighting trick." Techniques or attack combinations designed to get past an opponent's defenses.

Displace
Deflect an attack with your own attack/blow, so that it misses its target.

189

Displacements

There are four Displacements and they describe the breaks for the four basic guards: Crooked Strike breaks Ox, Crown Strike breaks Fool, Cross Strike breaks From the Roof, Squinting Strike breaks Plow.

Doubling

To strike the opponent from a binding position. Your own blade often comes between the opponent's sword and the opponent, making a defense almost impossible.

F

Feint

It is carried out as if you are about to attack a certain opening, in order to attack another vulnerable opening.

Feel

While in a binding position, to sense whether the enemy is hard or soft in the bind. Sense his intentions.

Flat

The flat, or broad side, of the blade.

Foible

The first third of the blade, beginning at the point and extending to the middle.

Fool

One of the six guards. The sword is held downward, the point is held in front of you pointing diagonally at the ground.

Forte

The last third of the blade from the cross guard to the middle.

From the Roof

One of the six guards. The sword is held with the cross guard at chin height or over the head. The point is aimed upward or slightly to the rear.

G

Garden Hoe

A swift sequence of vertical blows to the upper and lower openings, during which you step toward the opponent.

Guards

The basic stances. According to Liechtenauer there are four different guards, while Ringeck names six. They are: Fool, Plow, Ox, From the Roof, Barrier and Tail Guards. In many combat manuals there are even more, however most are variations of Ringeck's six basic guards.

H

Handwork

The combat itself—between the approach and withdrawal. The actual sword fight occurs during Handwork.

Hanging

Stance in which the point or the pommel "hangs" downward.

Hilt

The grip of the sword including cross guard, grip and pommel.

I

Iron Gate

A guard in which the point is placed on the ground in front of you. Similar to the Barrier or Fool Guard.

K

Key

A guard in which the hilt is held far back. The blade rests on the left arm, pointing forward. The hilt is held roughly in front of the right breast.

L

Long Edge

The edge of the sword that strikes the target in a normal blow. The edge that points away from the fighter when holding the sword normally in front of him.

Long Point

Also called "Long Guard." An additional guard, with the blade horizontal and the arms extended straight forward. The hands and blade form a line.

M

Master Strikes
According to Ringeck there are five Master Strikes: Crooked Strike, Strike of Wrath, Cross Strike, Crown Strike and Squinting Strike.

Meanwhile
Not "Before" or "After," but "Meanwhile" or "at the same time." Most important tempo in sword fighting, because it is the only safe one.

Measure
Distance. The term refers to the various distances between fighters during combat.

Middle-Cut
A left-to-right horizontal side cut at medium height.

Mutate
A Winding technique in which you thrust from the Ox position past the opponent's hands to his lower openings without losing blade contact.

O

On the Sword
To execute an attack from a bind. You work "on the sword."

Openings
The opponent's four openings. The first is his right side above the belt, the second is his left above the belt, the third is his right side below the belt and the fourth is his left below the belt. Also called Windows.

Over-Cut
Every blow that is struck from above.

Overrunning
A blow which reaches the opponent before his reaches you. For example a Crown Strike against the legs.

Ox
One of the six guards. The sword is held with the cross guard at eye level or higher, the point aimed at the opponent's face. Optimally place the thumb on the blade.

P

Place
An attack aimed at a certain body part.

Plow
One of the six guards. The sword is held with the grip at hip level, the point is aimed up and forward, toward the opponent.

Plunging Cut
A powerful strike, in which you advance and simultaneously strike from above with the short edge with crossed hands.

Point
The tip of the sword.

Push Through
A timed thrust whose target is between the opponent's hands and body.

R

Running In
To change from a near to a close measure. Usually followed by wrestling and/or throws. Running In is the beginning of wrestling on the sword.

Running Through
The attempt to pass the opponent's weapon and reach his back.

S

Set Aside
To simultaneously parry the opponent's blade while making a thrust—usually from the Ox or Plow.

Short Edge
Also called the "false edge." The edge of the sword that normally points toward the fighter when holding the sword normally in front of him.

Slice Off
To slice across the opponent's hands from below or above.

Snap
To execute a sudden movement of the blade from the bind and immediately strike the side of the opponent's blade. During the movement the pommel snaps forward and back.

Snap Off
To disengage from a bind by sliding or batting the blade away with a strong blow.

Squinting Strike
One of the Master Strikes. A downward cut with the short edge at the opponent's shoulder or neck.

Strike Around
To pull away after a blow for another to the opposite side.

Striking Through
To carry through a blow from below against the opponent's blade to the point that you separate from the bind and thrust at another opening.

T

Tail Guard
One of the six guards. The sword is held with the cross guard at hip level, the point is aimed down and back.

Talking Window
The blades are in a strong bind, and you wait for or determine the opponent's intentions.

Three Blows
Three blows in succession—an under-cut from the right, an under-cut from the left, followed by a powerful Crown Strike.

Three Wonders
The three components of sword fighting: the cut, the thrust and the slice.

Tick
A light strike with the weapon.

Twitch
Suddenly and abruptly change the direction of attack.

U

Under-Cut
Every blow that is struck from below.

Unicorn
The Unicorn is an end position after an under-cut, with the point aimed high. In the right Unicorn the arms are crossed.

V

Viper Tongue
A rapidly repeated sequence of thrusts over the opponent's hilt, during which a changing through movement is repeatedly indicated but never carried out, until the opponent becomes confused and leaves an opening for a thrust. The movement resembles the flicking tongue of a viper.

W

War
Winding, mutating, doubling, binding etc.—all the techniques that take place at relatively close quarters. The point is mainly used in the War position.

Wheel
To hold the sword with an outstretched right arm and execute a swift circular-motion of the blade in front.

Winding
Any turning of the blade while pressing on the opponent's blade in order to bring one end or the other of your sword (point or pommel) against him. There is a total of 24 Winds (1 x 2 x 3 x 4 + 24)" "One winding from two sides with three attacks to the four openings."

Withdraw
To disengage from the opponent and move out of range of his weapon. Usually after the combat has ended.